P9-CJC-344

Also by Art Buchwald

Lighten Up, George

Whose Rose Garden Is It Anyway?

I Think I Don't Remember

"You *Can* Fool All of the People All of the Time"

While Reagan Slept

Laid Back in Washington

The Buchwald Stops Here

Down the Seine and Up the Potomac

Washington Is Leaking

Irving's Delight

"I Am Not a Crook"

The Bollo Caper

I Never Danced at the White House

Getting High in Government Circles

Counting Sheep

The Establishment Is Alive and Well in Washington

Have I Ever Lied to You?

Son of a Great Society

And Then I Told the President

I Chose Capitol Punishment

Is It Safe to Drink the Water?

How Much Is That in Dollars?

Don't Forget to Write

More Caviar

Brave Coward

Art Buchwald's Paris

A Gift from the Boys

Paris After Dark

Art Buchwald's Secret List to Paris

LEAVING HOME

LEAVING HOME

a memoir

Art Buchwald

G. P. PUTNAM'S SONS
NEW YORK

G. P. Putnam's Sons
Publishers Since 1838
200 Madison Avenue
New York, NY 10016

Published simultaneously in Canada

Library of Congress Cataloging-in-Publication Data

Buchwald, Art.
Leaving home : a memoir / Art Buchwald.—1st American ed.
p. cm.
ISBN 0-399-13864-1
1. Buchwald, Art—Biography. 2. Humorists, American—20th century—Biography. 3. Americans—France—Paris—Biography.
I. Title.
PS3503.U1828Z47 1994 93-32755 CIP
814'.54—dc20
[B]

Printed in the United States of America
1 2 3 4 5 6 7 8 9 10

This book is printed on acid-free paper.

ACKNOWLEDGMENTS

Many people helped me in the writing of this memoir. Three I would particularly like to cite are Phyllis Grann, my publisher and editor of sixteen years; Neil Nyren, who cheerfully edited this book; and Jeannie Aiyer, my friend and assistant, who did the research, provided constant cheer-leading and invaluable advice, and questioned me unmercifully when the material made no sense to her. I am their humble servant.

INTRODUCTION

I am new at writing memoirs. It's probably the most egotistical project a person can undertake, but it does provide an opportunity to sum up the few years I've spent on earth in my own words.

At one point I called my friend Russell Baker and asked, "What do you do if you're discussing someone who was mean to you in your childhood and that person is still alive?"

He replied, "Change his name."

That's the advantage of an autobiography over a biography for someone like me—the subject has complete control over the book's contents. So the reader should not be surprised to find that I am the hero of all the stories, and I present a magnificent profile in courage.

I can't swear to every fact in this book, but I can vouch for the accuracy of the descriptions of people and events, both from my own memory and the memories of all those I talked to.

I conducted a number of interviews during my research. The

conversations from them were all recorded and the quotes I have used accurately reflect what was said. The quotes from my childhood conversations are different—they are nothing more than my own recollections of past events.

Many of the leading players in my story are gone. Some I miss because they helped me and were nice. I would love to have given them an autographed book. Others were not kind, and I find myself hoping they would still be alive so that I could strut my stuff in front of them.

The skeletons in my closet are not as frightening now, but they scared me as a child. And they affected me for life. I have never been into drugs or alcohol, because I was always afraid that by taking them I would lose my sense of humor. But I have had two serious clinical depressions, which may or may not be blamed on the events of my youth.

The book is dedicated to my three sisters, Alice, Edith, and Doris, who had similar childhoods; to my father, who loved us but was a victim of very bad luck; and to all the strangers who helped me get to where I am today.

I love you all.

LEAVING HOME

1

Mother and Pop

Shortly after I was born, my mother was taken away from me or I was taken away from my mother. This was done because she was mentally ill. She suffered from severe chronic depression, which required that she be committed to a private sanitarium. She never recovered and, eventually, when my father ran out of money, she was placed in a state hospital in upper New York for thirty-five years—the rest of her life.

The medical facts, as provided to me by the Harlem Valley State Hospital in New York, are as follows:

My mother was born in Hungary in 1893 and came to this country in 1906, where, with very little schooling, she went to work in a factory. In 1918 she married my father and then had four children.

The report said, "She was jolly and friendly until the age of thirty, when she suddenly became suspicious and imagined people were poisoning her food. She was admitted to the Westport Sanitarium on June 4, 1925, and was released on

August 20, 1925." (I was born on October 20, 1925, which meant that she was sick during the pregnancy.) "When her condition did not improve she was readmitted on February 18, 1926. She refused to eat and expressed paranoid ideas.

"The patient was transferred to Harlem Valley State Hospital, where she gradually regressed."

I never saw my mother, although she lived until I was in my thirties. When I was a child, they would not let me visit her. When I grew up, I didn't want to. I preferred the mother I had invented to the one I would find in the hospital. The denial has been a very heavy burden to carry around all these years, and to this day I still haven't figured it all out.

Early in life I had to explain her absence to strangers, as did my sisters. The easiest thing was to say she died giving birth to me. I don't know how many times I told this lie, but apparently every time I did I committed a form of matricide. She was dead as far as friends and strangers were concerned, but she was very much alive to me—sequestered away in a distant place I had never seen. The story was credible—but for most of my life I have lived in fear that someone would unearth my dirty secret and I would be severely punished for not having disclosed it.

When I grew up and I was in analysis in Washington, D.C., with Dr. Robert Morse, discussions about my mother took up quite a bit of our time. One of the reasons for this was that she turned up in so many dreams—watching me, following me, but never saying anything. I might escape her in the daytime but not when I slept.

In my dreams, she never helped. She just stared at me, as if to say, "Well?"

Although I had never seen her in person, I saw photographs. She looked very attractive, with brown hair, high cheekbones, and no-nonsense features. I perceived a stern look about her, though this could have been attributed to guilt. I sometimes felt that I would have been the recipient of a very disciplined, kosher upbringing had she not disappeared from my life at a very early age.

As the only boy in the family, I might have been spoiled by her. On the other hand she might have lowered the boom on me for trying to be a free spirit. I never knew what a mother was, so I couldn't imagine her holding me in her arms. Dr. Morse and I concluded that I was envious of people who did have real mothers, and when I acted out I wanted to prove that it didn't bother me.

During the various stages of my life, I often wondered if I was responsible for her illness and incarceration. After all, she was taken away at my birth, so who else could be blamed?

As with many children who never knew their mothers, I have been on a lifelong search for someone to replace her. The search has taken more time than my work, and although I know that I will never find a surrogate, I can't seem to stop looking.

In 1960, at age sixty-seven, she died. She had cancer of the liver. My sisters, Alice, Edith, and Doris, told me that they had gone to see her in the hospital when she was dying.

Alice said, "She looked very nice."

Edith's response was, "She didn't look nice—she looked awful."

"She looked a lot better than I anticipated."

"Well, you must have anticipated something really bad."

"She was dying of cancer. What did you expect?"

I asked them how long after that visit had she died.

"A month. I remember the hospital because a lot of patients were wearing crucifixes. Not little ones, big ones."

"I remember the hospital because it was so screwed up. Doris, who was a nurse, asked to see the records—and the doctor read from a document in front of him. It turned out that he was reporting on a different patient. When Doris pointed this out, he didn't even apologize. He just picked up another folder."

"Did you say anything to her when you saw her?"

Alice said, "I remember saying to her, 'Mother, I just want you to know that Poppa has been good to us.' She gave me a funny look and a smile. I don't know what the smile meant, whether it was, 'Is that so?' or something else."

There was a funeral for her in New York. I didn't make it because I was in Paris at the time. My sister Edith wrote me a letter telling me about Mother's death, the services, and the difficulty in finding a burial plot. The rabbi, who didn't know her, gave the eulogy, and twenty-five of our aunts and cousins, mostly on my father's side, showed up for the funeral.

I was shaken by the news. Since the funeral had taken place a week before the letter arrived, it was obviously too late for me to attend, and there was no need to go home. So even when she was buried, I did not see her.

I asked my sister Edith why she hadn't called or cabled me in Paris.

"The funeral was the next day—you couldn't have made it."

"How did you know that?"

"We weren't thinking."

My wife, Ann, told me that I walked into our dining room in Paris and sat down. She said, "What's wrong?"

I blurted out, "My mother died," and immediately started to cry. Ann came over and put her arms around me and said, "Don't tell me that you expected to get through this without crying."

When we grieve, tears and guilt get mixed together. My

sisters have always tried to console me by saying that, even if I had gone to see my mother, she wouldn't have known who I was. They said that I would have been as much a stranger to her as she was to me. This thought has helped, but sometimes, particularly at night, I think that I was a coward not to go and see her.

In spite of my never having seen her, she was very much a part of me. In 1963, I had a severe depression myself and was hospitalized. In my darkest moments in my room, I would cry, "I want my mommy, I want my mommy."

When I told my story to Dr. Morse the next morning, he said that he was not surprised. I had gagged up a whole lifetime of maternal deprivation.

In the beginning, there was my mother and father and my three sisters, Alice, Edith, and Doris. Being the youngest and the only son, I had the best of it. We lived in a rented house in Mt. Vernon, New York. I have always maintained that it was a white house just like the one George Washington lived in.

My father had come from Austria and arrived in this country when he was fifteen years old. He was five feet eight, and he had a gentle smile and a face framed by large protruding ears. Luckily, he was stocky and strong, because drapes are not light when you carry them around on subways or install them in someone's living room. That was his trade—lifting, hammering, and measuring curtains and drapes—for the greater part of his life.

The historians in my family are my sisters Alice Gordon and Edith Jaffe. Although they both have almost total recall, it doesn't follow that either of them recalls the same version of any event.

When I first started this book, they were very apprehensive. They were concerned that since the family had told so many tales for so long, my memoirs would raise issues which had been buried for years. They agreed to help me but that didn't mean they approved of what I was doing. My youngest sister, Doris, with whom I had lived for longer periods than the others, was not very helpful with details, maintaining she had blocked out her memories of childhood. I believed her.

My first debriefing with Alice and Edith took place in the Regency Hotel in New York.

I sat them on a couch and served them coffee. They were both nervous, tossing over in their minds what to tell me and what to hold back. My job was to play the role of the good detective and get them to spill the beans. The family closet was loaded with secrets. None of them were bad, but the information was privileged, and as Edith said as I turned on the tape recorder, it was "nobody's damn business."

"Tell me what you know about Pop," I said.

Between Alice and Edith I learned that Pop had left Europe in 1912 because he didn't want to serve in the Austro-Hungarian Army and die for the Hapsburgs. He had nothing against the royal family, but he didn't see much of a future out of making them happy. He was also anxious to escape a situation which was increasingly hostile to Jews.

My sisters had an interesting story on how we had acquired the name Buchwald. Our grandmother had been married to a man with the last name of Semel, who was a foreman on a large estate. It was a very good job, but he made the mistake of drinking water that had been contaminated with typhoid —so he died. Grandma Semel went to live with her in-laws, who were unkind to her—there were eight brothers and they all treated her very harshly—so, in anger, she returned to her own home and took back her maiden name, which was Buchwald.

I thought, "What a break. Who would have ever hired a columnist named Art Semel?"

I discovered that father's mother was not only strong but beautiful, with blonde hair and blue eyes, just like Aunt Molly, my father's sister. Grandma was religious, and when Pop emigrated to the New World, her last words to him were, "Don't marry one of the other kind."

Pop told my sisters that he had worked very hard to make money to come over here. He finally saved enough to buy a steerage class ticket, and he sailed from Rotterdam without knowing a soul. His most vivid memory of the trip was that because all the passengers were Jewish (and kosher), the crew stood on the bridge and kept tossing them herring out of barrels. He said he was sick from the herring and sick from the motion of the ship throughout the entire voyage.

My sister Alice maintained that Pop worked in a delicatessen in Chernowicz to earn the fare for the trip. Edith said, "They didn't have delicatessens in Chernowicz."

Alice became huffy. "Well it was *like* a delicatessen. They sold potato salad and pickles. Pop told me what he did to come over. He probably didn't tell Edith."

They said that Pop had had a little schooling in the old country. He could read and write German, which must have been the language of instruction. At the same time, he was fluent in Yiddish, which he either learned at home or in a Jewish school. What he didn't know was English.

His main concern on the ship was that he would not be admitted to the United States. It didn't matter how much herring you ate or how seasick you got, the American immigration authorities were very strict about who they accepted. If someone couldn't pass the physical, they shipped them back to where they had come from, which, for Pop, was a frightening idea. It was not so much returning home that scared him as having to repeat the same voyage again.

My father had told Alice that he wasn't that much in love with Ellis Island, mainly because he could see Manhattan from there—it was so near and yet so far away.

"What a joke!" I said. "Now he has a plaque there with his name on it." A few years ago Ellis Island began selling people brass name plates to place on a wall surrounding the island. It was a fund-raising gimmick to help renovate the buildings. For a fee, the name of any immigrant who passed through Ellis Island could be engraved on a plaque. The Buchwalds now have three plaques—one for Pop, one for Mother, and one for Uncle Oscar.

Since my father had been so determined to get off the island, Alice felt uncertain that he would have approved of remaining there permanently on a plaque.

I've been to Ellis Island and visited the wall where his name is inscribed. The plaque faces Manhattan, the place he hated and loved for almost seventy years.

I said, "Once he arrived in America, he never wanted to leave. In the fifties, when I was working in Paris, I offered him a trip to Europe and he turned me down with the curt response, 'I've already been there.' "

My father set foot in this country carrying a small bag which contained his only belongings. He looked up relatives of his stepfather named the Wuchers, who lived on the Lower East Side, and they helped him get started. After various jobs he ended up in a raincoat factory. Although he was declared an enemy alien when the United States entered World War I, he made it up to America by producing trenchcoats for our doughboys. We used to boast that if it weren't for my father's raincoats, the Kaiser would now be living in the White House.

I once asked him how he'd first learned his English, and he told me that he read the New York newspapers. He couldn't afford to buy them, so he picked them up from the seats in subway trains after other people had finished with them. The *Daily News* and *Daily Mirror* had priority because they ran so many photographs and were the easiest ones to read. The *Times* and *Herald Tribune* were the toughest, but he always made an attempt to read one every day.

His favorite New York paper, though, was the *Jewish Daily Forward,* because it was in Yiddish.

Edith said, "Every once in a while, after you were writing a column, your name appeared in the *Forward,* and it turned out to be a very big day for Pop because so many of his friends had seen it."

When he passed away, my niece, Nancy Gordon, found a certificate stating that Pop had earned an English literacy requirement in 1928, which enabled him to vote. He had become an American citizen in 1927. He never mentioned either occasion to me or my sisters.

World War I started, and father's mother died of flu, while being pursued by the Cossacks, or some other rotten guys. Pop's stepfather died a short while later. This left Uncle Oscar and Aunt Molly fleeing to Vienna. They were young orphans and were placed in a home financed by the Rothschilds. Pop did not know of their whereabouts until the war was over, and in 1918 he managed to locate them in the orphanage and brought them to the United States.

In the beginning, they lived with him and my mother. Meanwhile, before the war, my father had also brought over his older sister Sarah, who married a man named Charles Lampner, with whom she had three children, Eddie, Arthur, and Rosalind. Sarah was adored by everyone in the family and she died giving birth to Rosalind. The Lampner children also wound up as foster children, so their early lives were similar to ours.

Pop was very pleased when he managed to get Aunt Molly to America. Part of the family lore is that when she was sixteen, she went to school and became a political radical. When my father invited Aunt Molly to work in his shop, the first thing she did was organize his employees into a union. Pop couldn't believe that after all the sacrifices he had made, his own sister would do something like that to him. Aunt Molly, in turn, couldn't believe that my father employed "slave" workers.

Pop's best friend in the New World was Julius Gartner, a big, strong man who could have been a wrestler. Gartner was originally from Russia, and he and my father shared a loft when they went into business together. Gartner was like a brother, very supportive as Pop went from one misfortune to another. One time when my sister Doris was a baby, she was quite sick and needed many blood transfusions. The doctor at the clinic informed Pop that he would give no more transfusions to Doris unless he was paid in cash. Gartner, who was with my father, grabbed the doctor by the throat and told him that if he refused to give Doris blood he would be dead.

Gartner said, "You'll get your money, but don't take it out on the child." This story is why everyone in the family always liked him, even though he used to spit in our faces when he talked.

While my sisters seemed eager to talk about Pop, they were less willing to discuss my mother. It was the area that everyone, including me, had always considered off-limits.

Edith said that my mother had come from Hungary, but that we didn't know much more about her origins, except that her parents were Rebecca and Isaac Klineberger, and she had had a brother and three sisters.

"Somebody told me that she was brought over to the United States by an aunt and uncle," Alice added. "Pop met her through her relatives who lived in Brooklyn." They were married in June 1918 and, after my father finished with raincoats, my mother's uncle put him into drapes and slipcovers.

The marriage seemed all right at the beginning. My mother was quite religious and observed all the holidays. Alice claims that every time she accepted a piece of bread she had to say a prayer.

But there was mystery and darkness in the air. The girls said Pop found out that about five years before the marriage my mother had had a breakdown and had been sent back to Hungary for a cure. No one in Mother's family had told him about it. One of her brothers also had had a mental illness, and that had been a family secret as well. Would Pop have married her if he had known? No one in the family has ever had the answer to that question.

Pop did well financially until the Depression, when the bottom fell out. It wasn't just that business was lousy and people stopped buying curtains, but he was drowning in hospital bills. Mother was in expensive sanitariums, where the doctors kept promising that they could cure her. They couldn't. Doris and I were in a home run by nurses, as we both needed special care. Edith and Alice were in a boarding school until Pop ran out of money.

Edith said, "It must have been very painful for Pop to put Mother in the sanitarium. Before her illness, she was gregarious and social and an excellent cook—she entertained a lot.

She was strict with us, but affectionate, and we were very attached to her."

I said, "I wish I had known her."

Seven years after Pop married Mother, the family moved to Mt. Vernon, New York. "I was six years old," said Alice, "Edith was five, and Doris was two years younger." And then I came along.

My arrival on October 20, 1925, was an auspicious occasion—at least for Alice and Edith. I was born at home, which was not unusual in those days. What did make it different was that no one was with my mother except my sisters.

Alice said, "We were there for the whole thing, from the time you came out to when Mother cut the cord."

"That's heavy for two little girls," I admitted.

"I'll never forget it. I was six years old and I had to get the hot water."

Edith said, "Mother told me to go to Tante's house a few blocks away and tell her what was happening. You were already born and Mother had cleaned up the bed by the time Tante arrived. It was as if she did it all the time."

"Wasn't there any help?" I asked.

Alice said, "There was this cleaning woman who worked in the house, but I caught her stealing silverware, and I fired her."

Edith said, "You were only six, how could you fire anybody?"

"I did. I said, 'Get out, you're a thief,' and she went. I suspect that she had stolen a lot of things and wanted to leave the house before Pop came home. That's why Mother was alone with us."

I posed the tough question, "Was she depressive when she gave birth to me?"

"I don't think she was. She was out of it later, but when she had you she seemed normal."

"What kind of baby was I?"

"A small one—but you were beautiful."

"Was Pop notified?"

"Yes, he rushed home, and he had a big grin on his face because Mother had given birth to a boy."

"What happened next?"

"A relative came and took over. You were tiny and you had rickets because of a lack of calcium."

"How did you know all that?" I asked.

"I didn't until later, when they shipped you off to a hospital."

My sister Edith said, "I remember it, too. You didn't look too healthy."

"Were you frightened to see all this going on in your home?" I asked.

"I was scared silly. It's not something every kid gets to see when she is six years old."

"Was Mother cool, happy, or what?"

Alice said, "She didn't show much emotion. I remember this—she didn't scream once."

"Did you girls cry?"

"No, we were excited because we had a new baby."

"Does anyone recall if I was breastfed?"

"You weren't breastfed."

"No, I'm sure you weren't breastfed."

"Well," I said. "At least that explains my nail-biting."

I like to think that this unusual way of arriving in the world played an important part in my developing a positive attitude about life. Maybe it also influenced my decision at an early age that, if I was to survive, I would have to fend for myself rather than wait for help from others.

The big mystery was, exactly when was our mother taken away from us?

After much prodding, my sister Alice said that my mother had not been very well before I was born—and she was no better after my birth.

"You must have been two or three weeks old. Mother took off one day and left me in charge, and she didn't come back. There was nobody there but Edith and me. So I went out on the street and met Charlie Buchwald, our cousin, who was then in high school. I told him that Mother hadn't come home and you wouldn't stop crying because you were hungry. I asked him what I was supposed to do. He came into the house and fixed some food. I remember that."

"Do you remember if Mother acted strange often?"

"I couldn't say that, but I was six, so I didn't really know what acting strange was."

Apparently my mother had been disappearing almost every day while my father was at work, and no one knew where she went. The girls maintain that she was lucid at home, but she left them all day by themselves. So not long after my birth, the girls said, an ambulance arrived at the house. My father and Aunt Molly were there.

Alice said, "I'll never forget how they took her away. Aunt Molly kept yelling at us to stop crying. When I grew up, I realized that she had to yell to keep from breaking down herself."

At some point in the turmoil of those weeks, I was taken to the Heckscher Foundling Home because of my continuing problem with rickets (I'm still slightly bowlegged).

Edith said, "I don't remember Arthur being taken away."

Alice's response was, "Who said you should?"

My father could not take care of all of us and my mother's relatives offered to look after us—even adopt us—but that only infuriated my father, who told them, "I don't give my children away."

"The relatives wanted everyone but me," Alice said.

Edith nodded her head. "Even then they knew."

Without a mother, we all took on identities which carried us through the rest of our lives. Alice, being the eldest, assumed the role of mother and tried to take charge of us, which didn't work at all. She was the one who looked the most like my mother, and since we were adrift so much of our childhoods she felt it was her duty to boss us around.

Edith was gentle, much less assertive than Alice, and was very dependent on her older sister. Although they fought a lot as children, they clung to each other for dear life. They have never been separated, not as children, not as young women. They only went their own ways when they got married. They shared something which Doris and I did not—they had memories of our mother. For a short period they had known what it was like to live with their own parents.

Doris was very quiet and was far more sensitive about what was going on around her than I was. She influenced my attitudes toward the different places in which we lived. She didn't like any of them. Her goal was to get out of every home we were sent to, and she counted on me being her ally in this work. As soon as we were placed in a foster home, we would go to Doris' room after dinner and plot how to get out. She kept lists of war crimes to spring on the social worker on her next visit. I was less anxious to keep moving around, but Doris kept bringing up different reasons why we could not stay.

Our bedroom conversations went something like this:

"Did you see it?" she would ask me.

"See what?"

"She offered Lorraine seconds on the rice pudding and she didn't offer us any."

"I don't think she offered Lorraine seconds. Lorraine took them without asking," I told her. "Like she usually does."

"Why do you always take their side?"

She had me there. I said, "Because I never look for trouble."

"What if we say we never have any clean clothes to wear, and we always smell terrible in school and nobody will sit next to us."

"Why?" I wanted to know.

"So we'll get into a better home."

"What if it's worse than this one?"

She said, "Nothing could be worse than this one."

I played the role of knocking down all her escape plans. I had concluded that one home was as good as another if you adjusted to it.

Doris felt otherwise. She had decided at an early age that life was unfair. I heard her say many times, "If you don't let people know how you feel, they will walk all over you." I just thought it was safer to keep things to myself—I still do.

She had good reason to feel the way she did. Early in life, she was left outside in the cold and developed a serious infection in her leg which turned into osteomyelitis. Over the next three years she was in and out of a series of hospitals and there was even discussion about amputating the leg. My father would not hear of it. Her early years were not pleasant at all, and she suffered far more than I did. There was no hugging in her life. Come to think of it, there was none in mine either.

As brother and sister we got along well enough. Our biggest

disagreement concerned the fact that, since I was one year younger and a boy, she insisted on being my mother. I wanted no part of mothering from her or my other two sisters. I constantly reminded all of them that if I were looking for a mother, I wouldn't choose any of them.

Doris was very resentful of Alice and Edith, because she believed they were always getting the better deal. She was one of life's great comparison shoppers and measured how she was doing by how well other people were doing.

We came as a pair, and because of this close relationship I developed a guilt complex about not taking care of her. She went on to become a nurse and an army lieutenant, eventually married, and had a son who is now a successful lawyer. In spite of all this, I felt I should have done more. In childhood she had become my responsibility, just as I had become hers. I never shook it off even after I grew up.

I stayed in the Heckscher Foundation for about a year. I have no memory of it, but I'm okay today so I must owe them something.

Then somebody recommended that I be sent to a small boarding house for sick children in Flushing, New York, run by Seventh-Day Adventists. A German nurse named Mrs. Schneck was in charge of the home, and she occupied the house with her husband and two daughters, and eight to ten child boarders. When my sister Doris was discharged from the hospital, she was sent to the same place.

I lived there until I was five years old, and it played a vital role in my development. It was a large, warm house, set back on a generous piece of land with plenty of room for children to play. My memories of particular incidents from that time are rather dim, but I remember that they had a dog. There were several photos of me with him—including the one on the cover of this book—and he was shaggy and very friendly. But I have no recollection of his name.

My strongest impression of the home was the strict religious upbringing I received. The nurses were God's messengers on what constituted sin and what didn't. I am talking about serious sin now.

They practiced their religion faithfully, and they expected us to do the same. Eating meat, fish, and eggs was a sin. Dancing or listening to the radio was a sin. The German nurses filled my head and heart with hell and damnation, and if you broke the rules, their demons were waiting to shovel you into the fiery pit down below, somewhere near China.

I have no memories of the weekdays but I have total recall of attending church on Saturdays in New York on Riverside Drive. We were bundled up and taken on the trolley to Jamaica, and then the train into New York, changing many times, until we got off on Riverside Drive.

The church was enormous and had scenes depicting the life of Jesus on many of the windows. But it was the area around the altar that intrigued me the most. There was a stage, and below the stage was what I took to be a swimming pool.

I remember people standing in line to have the minister submerge their heads under the water. Baptism is very much part of the Seventh-Day Adventists' religion. I was fascinated when people were dunked into the water, and I was sure that it was being done against their will. I was constantly waiting for someone not to come up, but it never happened, which disappointed me very much. There was a little thrashing around, but once everyone dried off they looked very happy.

"Did you have any desire to want to dunk your own head in the water?" Doris once asked me.

"No, I didn't. That is the funny part of it. Somehow I knew I wasn't a Seventh-Day Adventist. I also knew that I didn't belong to the people who were taking me to church. Although they took care of all our physical needs, they showed no love or affection that I can recall. They scared me with all their religious dogma, and even though I attended the rituals I had no interest in becoming a member of the congregation and being drowned on stage."

During my sessions with Dr. Morse, I concluded that somebody had been messing around with my head during those early years and they left footprints on my brain. I have spent almost as much time on the Seventh-Day Adventists in my analysis as I have on my mother. I am willing to bet that this place was responsible for many of my hang-ups.

For many years I had dreams from that period. A blurred likeness of the devil kept popping up, and it wasn't one of those friendly devils you see on canned ham salad—he was one mean son of a bitch. I conjured up all forms of sin from my childhood. I once had a bull with four horns attack me in a dream because I had eaten steak for dinner that night. To this day, I can't eat fish with scales on them. I have made my peace with shellfish and meat, but there is still a tiny Seventh-Day Adventist inside of me screaming to get out every time I make a pass at a tuna fish sandwich.

Apart from the religious indoctrination, my memories of this home were not unhappy ones. There was no school and no pain with regard to my treatment for rickets. Besides my sister, my cousin Rosalind was also there with a serious ailment. The nursing care must have been effective, because I recovered completely from rickets and Doris recovered from her osteomyelitis.

Our reward for attending church was that we were permitted to run across to the park overlooking the Hudson River and watch the ocean liners sailing by. I loved it and early on dreamed of sailing on one. It was the best part of going into New York.

My father visited us almost every Sunday, alone or with my sisters or my Uncle Oscar. Oscar was our favorite uncle—he was Pop's youngest brother, and he always had time for us. Oscar was a bachelor all his life, although he was quite handsome and could have made someone a great husband. This is just conjecture on my part because I knew nothing of his private life.

What made Oscar such a romantic figure to us later on was that he worked as a waiter at the St. Moritz Hotel. At that time it had one of the fanciest restaurants in the city, and its clientele included some of the biggest names in New York. Whenever we saw him, which was about once a month, we would ask, "Uncle Oscar, who was in the restaurant last week?"

Oscar would reply, "Walter Winchell. He's a lousy tipper, but you know who is worse? Nick Kenny's brother." Nick Kenny was a radio columnist for the *Daily Mirror* and well known in those days. It turned out that his brother not only threw his weight around with Uncle Oscar but also stiffed him. To this day my family hates Nick Kenny for the way his brother treated Oscar.

What made it so wonderful was that Uncle Oscar never failed to give us names—famous names who were tight spenders. We took this information to school to pass around to the other kids.

"Cary Grant is one of the stingiest people in the world."

"How do you know that?" one of the kids would ask us.

"My Uncle Oscar waited on him at the St. Moritz. Grant left a quarter."

"Who else?"

"You want to know who? Bing Crosby. He doesn't throw money around either."

Oscar always listened in as he served, hoping to make a killing in the stock market. One time he overheard a tip that Bernard Baruch was giving to his luncheon partner. Oscar rushed to the phone, called his broker, and in the following week lost his shirt.

My sisters were faring no better than Doris and I were. They had started life with a home and parents, and then it was all swept away. When they were five and six, they had been enrolled in a boarding school in Pelham. It was posh and included children whose parents were involved with the theater. But then Pop's business had turned sour, and they were withdrawn and placed in a home called the Shield of David.

Pop was trying to do a balancing act all on his own. He visited my mother in the sanitarium, then checked in at the Shield of David, and finally came out to Flushing to see us. It couldn't have been fun for him, and when I look back, I wonder how he handled all the body blows. Every time his business went down, he had to deal with all the obligations. My mother's sanitarium, located in Westport, was extremely expensive, and when he fell behind in the payments, he had to move her.

Finally, because of his financial woes, he had to take her out of the last one and she was sent to Harlem Valley State Hospital—and that is where I never saw her.

My father's visits to Flushing were epicurean events. He brought his own lunch, which he shared with Uncle Oscar and sometimes with Alice and Edith. It consisted of delicatessen food—corned beef, pastrami, chicken, and herring. The nurses went crazy every time Pop opened his package. But my father was oblivious to what he was doing to the vegetarian household, and he could never understand why we didn't eat any of the treats he brought for us. Doris and I used to watch with fascination as Pop and Oscar ate their corned beef, and we waited for God to send a thunderbolt to strike them dead. My sister and I concluded that both my father and my Uncle Oscar had some magical powers to ward off the Lord's vengeance on meat eaters.

I've always wondered what Pop must have been thinking, seeing us in this Seventh-Day Adventist setup. He was not a very orthodox Jew, but he went to the synagogue and might be called a religious person. This life for his children could not have been to his liking. He knew that we were getting large doses of religion and that we were attending church regularly. I've thought about it a lot, and the only thing I can figure out is that he had no other choice. Since the nurses were taking good care of us, he must have believed that no harm could come from our not being raised in a Jewish home.

I asked my sister Alice why Pop kept us in the home for so long. Alice said he didn't realize how serious the religious part of our health care was. "When did he find out?" I said.

"When you and Doris started singing 'Jesus Loves Me.'"

"What did he say?"

"He said, 'Time to go.'"

Soon after, Doris and I were told by the nurses that we were to leave. I didn't know what to make of it. What did I do wrong that they no longer wanted me? Where could I go, since this was my only home? Who could change their minds and let me stay?

I remember the departure very well because Doris and I

didn't want to leave, and Pop had a very difficult job getting us out of the house. I held on to the screen door, and Doris hid in the backyard. The two of us were dressed up as if we were going to church and we had our two small bags packed.

In spite of his Sunday visits, my father was still a stranger to us, and therefore I couldn't understand what he was doing dragging us away.

I was five years old and this was the third home from which I had been taken away. The first was in Mt. Vernon, where I had been born; the second was the Heckscher Foundation; and now this—all by the age of five. I was certain that I was being taken advantage of.

The nurses assured us that we could come back and see them anytime we wanted to. We had few toys—I had a duck and Doris a bear. We didn't know our destination, but when we got to Jamaica after forty-five minutes on the trolley, we were still crying. My father kept telling us that everything would be all right, but we had no idea what he meant by that. I recall one particular incident from that day. Because of all the tears, he decided to take us to a movie and calm us down. He couldn't have come up with a worse idea, because it had been drilled into us from infancy by the Seventh-Day Adventists that movies were your ticket straight to hell. As he tried to drag us into the theater to see Laurel and Hardy, we were fighting to get out. We caused such a fuss that the manager gave my father his money back and told him to take us to the movie down the street—presumably a hated competitor. That's how I remember it.

A word about Dr. Morse. I first went to him in 1962, after I had moved to Washington from Paris. I was suffering from the beginnings of my first depression and he tried to treat me so that I wouldn't have to go into the hospital. After a year, my condition worsened and I was eventually admitted to Sibley Memorial Hospital in Washington. He told me later he was unhappy that he had failed to prevent it, but I never held it against him.

What made him unique among the psychiatrists I have known is that he stretched out on his couch and the patient sat in the chair. Morse would stare at the ceiling as he listened to my story. Occasionally he would nod his head—but he rarely looked at me.

When I told him something, he would say, "How did you feel about that?" or, "How do you feel about that now?"

The first time it came up was when I told him about leaving the Seventh-Day Adventist home. He said, "How did you feel?"

I replied, "It didn't bother me."

He stared up at the ceiling and said nothing.

I waited, and when he didn't respond, I said, "Maybe it bothered me a little. I mean, after all, it was the only home I knew and I was being pulled out of it, which was a real crappy deal if you ask me."

More silence.

I continued, "I know that I was looking for someone to save me, like the nurses, but they didn't do anything. Doris didn't look too joyful either. It would have been different if we were unhappy in the place, but it wasn't bad at all."

"How did you feel about your father?"

"He did what he had to do."

I kept wondering what Morse saw on the ceiling.

Then I blurted out, "He didn't have to do it. He didn't have to take us out of there. We never really believed in Jesus."

"Have you ever forgiven your father for putting you in all these homes?"

"Of course. He couldn't help it."

The chair seemed terribly uncomfortable. "Okay, so maybe I was mad once in a while, but after all you can't go blaming everyone for your own life. Maybe I wouldn't have been a writer or a funny man if I had stayed in one place as a child. My father was okay and he was doing the best for all of us. I loved him, and while we couldn't show affection for each other, I'm sure he loved me. What's the next question?"

Withdrawing from the home in Flushing was the next step of my nomadic life. As I changed shelters, I became convinced that I would always be on the move. I adjusted to the shifts—first with tears, but, as I grew older, with a smile. I never let on how frightening the moves were to me. When I was small I kept trying to figure out who I belonged to. My father appeared regularly, but he never stayed. The orphanage and the foster homes I lived in were some sort of halfway houses, and no matter how nice the people were, I felt like an intruder using one of their bedrooms.

I was never mistreated. I went along with everything because I had no choice.

After Flushing, Doris and I were taken to the Bronx. Some distant relatives boarded us for a price, and we found ourselves trapped in a semi-tenement in the city. It was a cultural shock after the fields of Queens. Doris and I hated the noise and smells and everyone living on top of each other. I hardly knew the people who had taken us. I don't even recall them speaking to us.

It turned out to be a short stay, because not long after our arrival I was struck by an automobile. I was running for a ball in the street, and the vehicle hit me. The driver put me in his car and took me to the hospital, and I had five stitches sewn over my eye. I still have a scar. It's my only souvenir from the Bronx.

After that, my father decided that this particular part of the Bronx was not the place for Doris and me. That's how we wound up in the Hebrew Orphan Asylum.

2

The Hebrew Orphan Asylum

I am not certain how Pop found the Hebrew Orphan Asylum. Gaining admission to the HOA was harder than getting into Princeton. They didn't take just anybody. My father had to appear before a judge with us, since it was required that we be declared neglected children by the court before we would be remanded to the home. This was a bad rap for him, because we weren't neglected. But before the judge would sign us in, he had to have evidence that my father was a lousy parent.

I know all of this because, several years ago, the Jewish Welfare Board of New York contacted me and asked me to speak at the 150th Anniversary of the HOA. I said that I'd do it, but there was a fee involved.

They were surprised that I would charge and asked me what the fee was.

I said that I wanted my records. I knew that they had kept complete records of me, because a social worker visited us every month in our foster homes from the time we entered the HOA when I was six to the time I left at fifteen.

The man was horrified. "I can't do that," he said. "The records are sealed."

"Unseal them," I told him. A few days later, the story of my childhood as written by a dozen or so social workers was delivered. It's an interesting document, particularly if you are the person they are writing about. How many people in this world have had complete strangers keeping track of their childhoods? The records reveal that at the court hearing, the judge asked my father, "How much can you afford to pay weekly or monthly for your children's support?"

My father told him, "When business is good, I make twenty dollars a week. But business is bad now and I only make six or seven dollars. The reason I want to put my children in the Hebrew Asylum is that I live in one room and I don't have any place for them. Up until now I have been paying to keep the children in private homes, but I can't afford it anymore. I would like to have them committed to the Hebrew Orphan Asylum, but I do not want them put up for adoption. When my business gets better, I'll take them back."

The judge asked, "What about your relatives? Can't they take them?"

My father replied, "They won't unless I pay them."

The judge accepted Pop's petition and recommended we be placed in the HOA.

The records continued, "After the hearing, Judge Young committed Alice, Edith, Doris, and Arthur to the Hebrew Orphan Asylum and placed the father under an order to pay $2.50 a week for each child."

But things were so bad for Pop during the Depression that

he couldn't make the $2.50 payments. Here is a page from the HOA Records some time after we were placed in the home:

> Mr. Buchwald was queried as to when he would pay what he owed to the Institution. He appeared at the office by appointment. He went into a detailed discussion of his financial condition, which was not good.
>
> He said that due to conditions in the upholstery business, he had been making only $5 or $6 a week. He is self-employed and hopes that when the season begins at the end of August he might earn $25 or $30 weekly. He said that things should get better when the World's Fair came to New York.

I guess you could say that report sums up my father's business affairs in the thirties. It appears that during the Depression not too many New Yorkers were putting their money into drapes and curtains.

Pop prospered for a few years making blackout curtains for businesses and the government during the Second World War. But after the war ended, he lived on the edge. In the fifties, when I came to New York on home leave from Paris, I asked him how much money he owed. He mumbled a figure I couldn't hear. I then asked him how he kept going, and he said he borrowed from the loan sharks on Sixth Avenue. Then he repaid them at enormous interest. I was shocked but he just said, "Everyone in New York does it. The *momsers* leave me alone because I always pay them back."

There were other financial obligations involved with doing business in New York. Pop had to pay the fire inspector; he had to pay the cops and other civil servants. His bankers were mobsters. Despite what the movies tell you, the sharks make most of their loans to legitimate business people who need cash to tide them over until they are paid. The banks will not loan to people who are struggling, so desperate businessmen take the money from anybody they can. There are more people in New York like my father than like Ralph Lauren, who can get anything he wants by stopping at a Chase Manhattan office at tea time.

When I heard about Pop's bankers, I made other arrangements for him to get capital. He was reluctant to accept it. But he finally did.

It was typical of our relationship. He wanted no favors from me, and early in life I could not accept any from him.

With all his problems, Pop was a devoted father. If he didn't care about us, and if he hadn't made an effort to see that we were okay, he would have had a much easier life. I've thought back on his years and wondered if he had many days of peace. The only good side of his economic woes was that his firm, the Aetna Curtain Company, was not worth passing on to the next generation. If it had been, I would have wound up in the curtain business. I cringe when I imagine a sign on a window—Aetna & Son. The son would have been me.

Pop's was one of the millions of hard-luck stories of the thirties. He was responsible for four kids, at the mercy of the Jewish Social Service, and flat broke. If he was depressed, he hid it. He had a smile on his face almost all the time, so no one knew what was going on inside. The same has always been true with me, so the smile must be in the genes.

The records from the HOA testify to the fact that my father was a very caring man, and he was constantly consulted on our welfare by the social workers and foster parents. Every report indicates that he was involved in the decisions in our lives. The foster parents appealed to him when we weren't obeying, and I believe they respected him.

He never yelled nor did he lay a finger on any of us. I never heard him getting into a fight, and I never saw him violent. My sisters report otherwise. Alice told me that she once saw Pop throw a sewing machine across the length of his loft.

Edith also remembered the incident. She said that the machine had broken down, which meant that he couldn't get the order done, and so he just picked it up and threw it.

He ate most of his meals in dairy restaurants, and God knows what he ordered, because he went to the doctor once, and the doctor said he was suffering from malnutrition.

All the time we were in foster homes, we met Pop every Sunday in Jamaica—the most convenient place for him to see the four of us.

As far as I can remember, he always kept the date. Doris and I were living together and invariably arrived first and stood in front of the Merrick Theater at three o'clock. Pop came on time, but Alice and Edith were always late.

This used to make Doris and me very angry.

"They never come on time," she'd say.

I agreed. "They just think they're better than us."

Pop would say, "Maybe something happened."

Doris: "Nothing happened. They just want to prove that they can come anytime they want to."

Finally, the girls would show, anywhere from fifteen to forty minutes late. They would blame each other for their tardiness. I followed Doris' lead and refused to talk to them for at least ten minutes.

This was when I saw my father and had the most contact with him. I accepted the fact that he was my father, but I wasn't too sure exactly what that meant. He took me to movies and bought me ice cream, but I knew that by seven o'clock I would get on a bus, wave, and not see him again for another week. Our relationship was so different from those of my friends and their fathers.

I only became introspective about what was going on when I was writing this book. On the occasions that I saw him, I remember that he was extremely quiet. He didn't have much choice, because the four of us saved all of our feuds with one another for the moment we saw him.

I might tell Pop, "Doris took my school bag and she won't give it back."

"It wasn't your school bag—it was mine—yours had mustard all over it."

"I hate her," I would say. "I wish you would find a different foster home for her."

Edith and Alice had their own squawks. "You're wearing my blouse," Edith might say.

"You're wearing my stockings."

"Pop, tell her to leave my stuff alone."

Pop's response usually was, "You dasn't fight."

As I look back, it's remarkable how protective we all were of him. We knew that times were tough, so the four of us made a pact. We would either attend a first-run movie in Jamaica, of which there were three or four, and not eat much afterward, or we would go to a third-run film and gorge ourselves in the cafeteria. For all our fighting and arguing, everyone kept this part of the bargain.

Over the years, the girls continued to be protective. I was told not to bother him with bad news. His daughters were loving and caring, but they never shared any important aspect of their lives with him in case it would "disturb" him. He, in turn, kept his own counsel.

He didn't drink, except for one schnapps before he went to bed. When it came to customer relations, he had a sharp tongue. If someone complained about the order, he told the lady to take her business to his competitor, which he said was Macy's.

He had nowhere to go at night, so he not only provided curtains but listened to his customers' problems. People considered him part of the family, and many times his customers would invite him to join them for dinner. He was a storyteller and had many good tales to relate. When my column became successful, he talked about me. To make sure no one missed my columns, he carried them around in his coat pocket.

The only thing that kept Pop from being more social was that he owed everybody money. He was in debt to all our relatives, particularly the ones on my mother's side of the family. He owed the various orphanages and hospitals, and he never could get even with business acquaintances. He was constantly evading the people from whom he borrowed.

Pop battled the city every day. Once he told me he was held up on the street at midnight in front of his loft, and he said to the robber, "This is not a good thing for you to do. I don't have any money and if you get caught you will have to go to jail. If you want money, stick up someone on Park Avenue." The man shook his head and walked away.

Whenever he had to deliver an order, it meant using the subway. He had to carry the drapes and slipcovers on and off the trains and then hang them in the customers' homes. He felt that he was in a constant war with the subways. He once told me, "There are two kinds of people who ride the subway—those who push and those who get pushed. People who push get to live a lot longer than those who get pushed."

This sage advice has stayed with me through all the years.

Whenever I take the New York subway, which is rare, I observe the passengers—the ones who shove and the ones who are shoved—and I don't have to know any more about them.

My father didn't present me with golden nuggets of advice every day. We never said a lot to each other. I avoided telling him too much, because he thought that all my ideas were weird, and he said so. Since I got no encouragement from him, I just clammed up. In going over the relationship, I don't think I ever knew him well. There was no intimacy.

The subject we never, ever discussed was my mother. Not once did her whereabouts come up. He may have purposely tried to keep the shame of the illness from me. I never asked any questions. The girls brought up the fact that they knew where she was and they speculated on how well she was. But between my father and me, it was as if she never existed.

He never told me any stories about her. I know she was a subject of conversation with people like Aunt Molly and Uncle Oscar, but our relationship was such that her condition was a forbidden subject.

He had other problems with me as well. For example, I refused to be bar mitzvahed. The decision hurt him terribly. It's impossible for a Jewish father to explain to friends and relatives why his son isn't bar mitzvahed.

The declaration took place on a Saturday morning, when I was in his loft in New York.

I told him, "I don't want to be bar mitzvahed."

"Why not?" he demanded angrily.

"Because I don't want to go to Hebrew School at three when I finish my regular school. I never get a chance to play."

"It's for a short while. You learn some Hebrew, you make a nice speech, and everyone gives you a present. It's no big deal."

"I don't want to do it."

He was stumped. What could he do? He couldn't even cut off my allowance, because I wasn't getting one. Bribery wouldn't work. Appealing to the foster parents or the social worker was futile.

He said more in sadness than bitterness, "So don't get bar mitzvahed."

At this point, a good Jewish son would have said, "Okay, I've changed my mind."

I didn't. I'm not sure how he handled the explanation with his friends. I heard him tell my sisters that I went into a synagogue in New York with him and was bar mitzvahed by a rabbi, because I didn't want all the pomp and ceremony that went with the usual celebration.

I've thought a lot since then about why I made such an issue of refusing to go along with the bar mitzvah. The only reason I can give is that I was very mad at my father for what had been done to me, and since it was so important to him, I made the decision not to do it.

Besides the bar mitzvah debacle, I also hurt Pop when I ran away from home and enlisted in the Marine Corps. My sisters said he paced the floor night after night. It was only after I had my own son that I realized how painful my running away must have been for him.

After he found out where I was, he carried a picture of me in my Marine uniform in his wallet to show to everyone. He never was able to say to me how very pleased he was with my career.

The highlight for him was when I wrote a play called *Sheep on the Runway* and my name was in lights above the title on the Helen Hayes Theatre on Broadway. It was a gala opening which included Mayor John Lindsay, Ben Bradlee, Vince Lombardi, Edward Bennett Williams, Ethel Kennedy, and a cast of thousands.

My wife, Ann, and I greeted everyone, from my three sisters and their families, to a group of kids I went to grade school with in Hollis, New York—they were called the "Happy Girls." They bought out the second balcony and announced to one and all that they were my fan club.

I never saw my father happier than that night. He hadn't met many of my friends, and they were pleased to shake hands with him and say nice things about me out of my earshot.

After the opening, everyone went to Sardi's, where I hosted the party of my life. The reviews were mixed, but it didn't matter. I was having a great time. I said to my father at some point, "Pop, is it okay if we count this as my bar mitzvah?"

He smiled.

My father keeps popping up in strange places. Recently, I was in Bergdorf Goodman and asked a matronly lady for change to make a telephone call. She said to me, "I'm going to give it to you, not because you're a big shot, but because your father made my drapes for me. They're still hanging in the bedroom."

Another time I met a taxi driver who claimed to have driven my father on his jobs, although I had always understood he only used the subway.

I guess the weirdest thing that happened to me after my father died was when I was lecturing in Long Beach, California. After I finished my talk, I went back to the hotel and found a telephone message asking me to call a certain number. I did, and the woman who answered told me that she was the daughter of my father's girlfriend. This knocked me for a loop. She wasn't lying. She described him in detail and told me how he used to talk about us all the time. She confirmed that he carried my clippings in his pocket and showed them to her and her mother. She told me he was a father to her, too.

I had mixed feelings about the call. Part of me was happy that Pop had had a lady friend to share his life with—the other part of me felt a sense of betrayal. He was our father, so why was he devoting any of his time to someone else? I also tried to picture him as a visitor in someone else's home. For all our differences, the thought bothered me that I had shared him with people I didn't know.

I asked the caller if we could meet, but she said no. She just wanted to touch base.

After hanging up, I thought about the conversation. The liaison meant that my father had had more of a life than just working and sleeping in one room in a Bronx apartment. It also meant that someone besides us had cared for him.

That night, although it was three in the morning in the East, I called my three sisters and told them the news. They claimed that they'd known he had someone, but they didn't know who she was.

When my father died, I wrote a eulogy for him. I had gone to the funeral home with my best friend, Ben Bradlee, and Harry Dalinsky, a druggist who was also a close friend. They had both flown up from Washington to be with me. I handed my eulogy to the rabbi before the services. I knew what he planned to do. He was going to get up and say a bunch of crap for his twenty-five dollars and my father's entire life would have been a waste. The rabbi was reluctant to use my words and in the anger of the moment, I said, "You didn't know my father, and he didn't know you. If he did, he would have said, 'Don't let that guy say anything about me. He has no idea what he's talking about.' "

Bradlee squeezed my shoulder and said, "Atta boy." And when the eulogy was spoken, it was my words the rabbi used.

• • •

The Hebrew Orphan Asylum was founded in April 1860 by Jewish charities in New York City. Over the years, it moved several times, and finally established itself at 135th Street and Amsterdam Avenue across from the Lewisohn Stadium at the City College of New York. It was an institution in the true sense of the word—its outward appearance was forbidding-looking and not too hospitable when approached by a six-year-old for the first time. It housed boys and girls who stayed there until they were seventeen or eighteen. Few children qualified as real orphans—most had either a mother or a father or both. They were there either because they had been abandoned or because someone could not take care of them. In addition to the children actually living in the institution, a segment of the population was boarded out in foster homes. I don't know what the test was to remain in the HOA versus being a foster child.

I can't say which was better, since most of my youth was spent as a foster child. Some of the homes were good and some weren't too hot, as the foster parents were more interested in the money they received from the HOA than in the children. The HOA kids hated the words "orphan asylum," so they referred to the home as "The Academy."

The head of it was an imposing figure named Lionel Simmons, who ruled from 1919 to 1941, and under him the home produced a number of solid as well as distinguished citizens. Among the alumni were teachers, athletes, scientists, lawyers, doctors, war heroes, and many who made fortunes in business. One of the reasons the alumni record was so good was that the home had a team of volunteer psychiatrists and paid social workers to help those who might be in trouble. Except for the shame of being in an "orphanage," the home could have been considered a very proper prep school. The girls and boys leaned on each other in a world that was very confusing to most of them. Some married others who had been in the home.

As Hyman Bogen wrote in his book *The Luckiest Orphans,* when the kids were discharged from the HOA they had nowhere to go but up.

There is even an alumni society but it is fast disappearing since the HOA closed its doors in 1941. The HOA building was torn down during World War II to make room for a public school. During its existence, it is estimated, 35,000 children passed through the institution.

Many times I have run into the children of people who were in the HOA and, knowing that I was there, they want details. Sometimes their parents have spoken about the place, other times they have remained silent. For these children of HOA alumni, the asylum is very much part of their roots. They are searching for its secrets in order to help them better understand their parents.

When it moved the children to Pleasantville, the HOA became part of history. Pleasantville is a different institution—neither better nor worse—but different. It's modeled after Boys Town. There are bungalows, and the children have a "mother" and "father" living with them.

Even though my stay in the brick building was not very long, it left its mark on me—along with the ones I acquired when I went to my foster homes.

The worst part of being placed in the HOA was that Doris and I didn't know we were going there. My sisters said that our Uncle Oscar was the one who told them they were being put into the home. But Pop said nothing to the two of us.

Alice said, "I don't think Pop had the nerve."

Edith added, "He must have been more upset than we were."

Alice told me, "Oscar was very gentle. He explained that Pop had no choice."

There is a subway station at 137th Street and Broadway, and after coming out onto the street with my three sisters, I started the long, steep climb up the hill to Amsterdam Avenue. Pop was holding on to Doris and me, and we were pulling and tugging in the opposite direction. Uncle Oscar was holding on to Alice and Edith.

I was crying and so were my sisters. The Hebrew Orphan Asylum looked like a giant castle out of medieval times. All it lacked was a moat. It loomed above us, and there was no doubt in our minds that it would suck us up, and we would never be heard from again. Poor Pop, he kept picking us up and dumping us into one home after another.

I'm sure I said to myself, "What the hell is going on?"—or words to that effect.

Every child's arrival at the HOA was different. My cousin, Eddie Lampner, his brother, Arthur, and sister, Rosalind, were brought to the home at a different time. I once asked Eddie if the HOA didn't scare the hell out of him when he first saw it. He said that it might have, but he had had a previous experience with another orphanage, so this one looked like a piece of cake.

Eddie told me, "I was four years old. My mother had just died and my father had put my brother and me on a Long Island Rail Road train in Brooklyn. My father said, 'Sit here, I'll be right back.' Meanwhile, he went to talk to the conductor and then disappeared. He didn't return. The train left the station, and I was screaming and crying and beating on the glass. We went all the way to Far Rockaway before the conductor put us off and some people from an orphanage picked us up. They tell me that I didn't speak for four months."

Our arrival at the HOA wasn't that bad, but my sisters and I were dragged kicking and screaming into the front door. Pop and Oscar took us into a large reception hall, where they left us to be processed. They kissed us, and then they left. The four of us were very confused. We heard bells, and voices in offices. The halls were long and the ceilings high. Doris and I clung tightly to each other. After we sat on a bench for a short period, a stern woman separated me from my sisters. I was to go into the boys' isolation section and they were to go into the girls' dormitory. The last thing Edith said to me was, "Don't sit on the toilet seats."

That made me yell my head off.

Without intending to, my father had left me in a warehouse.

I was inspected for lice and a doctor checked every orifice in my body. After the physical, they took me to another office for a battery of psychological tests. I was so afraid I would flunk them that I kept looking at the lady before I put the blocks in the holes. In the boys' quarantine section there were bunk beds, and I was told to remove all my clothes. These were replaced with the HOA issue—itchy woolen uniforms and nightgowns. For some reason I recall that the pajama shirts reached down to my ankles.

The only good thing I remember about the day was that someone gave me jelly sandwiches and hot chocolate. The first night was the toughest. My father was gone, my sisters had disappeared. They told me I spent late afternoon looking out the window hoping Pop and Oscar would return.

I was told to get ready for bed by eight o'clock. I recall hearing a bell ringing. I jumped into bed, and I was shaking.

When the lights went out, the counselor came in with a flashlight and said, "Who is awake?" I didn't say anything. Then he asked, "Who is asleep?" and I raised my hand. He yelled, "Dummy," and kicked the side of my bunk as hard as he could. The lesson stayed with me for the rest of my life. I have never raised my hand to tell anyone I was asleep again.

The HOA was an institution of bells. They rang to get us up—they tolled for our meals and when to say our prayers and when to go to sleep.

Many years later, at a dinner in Lionel Simmons' honor, one of the HOA "boys" told how Simmons made them do things by the numbers when they went to bed: 1, jacket off; 2, sit on bed; 3, right shoe off; 4, left shoe off; 5, right stocking off; 6, left stocking off; 7, pants off; 8, clothes off; 9, go to bed; 10, in bed, eyes shut. The monitor would count to 300, and if you weren't asleep, all hell would break loose.

My father visited us every other day, which made things easier. My sisters visited me in the boys' wing as much as they could. They were concerned about me because I had become very quiet and had lost my energy. I wouldn't say anything about what was bothering me. I didn't understand why I had to be quarantined, because I hadn't done anything. In quarantine I watched from my window at the children playing in the yard. Most of them were older than me and I was very frightened about how I would fit in with the group. From what I could see of them, they were constantly wrestling with each other and kicking one another in the bottom. The future for me did not look good.

After two weeks, I was released and placed in the main boys' dormitory.

"Who are you?" one would ask.

"Arthur," I responded.

"Do you pee in your bed?"

"No," I responded.

"Everybody named Arthur pees in his bed."

"Don't either."

"Do too. You want to fight?"

"No. I don't want to fight."

"Are you really a girl?"

That's the way the dialogue went. I wasn't welcomed into the group, and I wasn't permitted to say anything, so I shut up. After a while I was left alone. I felt locked up. I couldn't relate to anyone there, and I saw less and less of my sisters.

One day recently, Alice remarked, "You never showed any anger about the situation."

"From what I can remember, I think that I was more puzzled than angry. I had no inkling of what I was doing in this building and I had no idea how long I would stay there. I longed for the peace of the Seventh-Day Adventist home." That turned out to be one of my biggest secrets at HOA. I had no idea what the kids would do to me if they found out I had prayed to Jesus.

My mind was whizzing along. I realized that I had to adjust to the place, at least until I was old enough to run away.

I had been in the HOA for two months and one day when I was called into a receiving room with my three sisters. They scrubbed us up so we would look better, in case someone wanted to take us home. I sat on the wooden bench, just happy to be with my sisters.

"Did they dress us nice?" I asked the girls during our talk at the Regency.

"No, why would they dress us nice?" Alice said. "We weren't up for adoption."

A middle-aged woman with glasses and wearing a large-brimmed hat and a double-breasted suit came in with a young man in his twenties. She was very businesslike and examined us as she would a Friday night chicken. She was smiling, though I had no idea what she had to do with me. Finally, she said, "How would you like to live with me?"

I replied, "I don't eat meat and I don't eat fish."

She said, "Well, we'll soon change that." Instead of protesting, I just looked down at my shoes.

As far as I was concerned, this woman was one more stranger asking me dumb questions. But she was also possibly my only ticket out of the HOA. I thought that it wouldn't hurt to be nice to her, just in case she had something to do with my freedom.

Her name was Stella Morais, and then she talked to my sisters, who were thinking the same thing as I was. If this lady wanted to take us out of the HOA, she was welcome to do it.

She said to me, "You're going to be my foster child."

I just smiled and nodded my head.

Her son Harold said, "I'll teach you how to play baseball and stickball." He was a dapper, good-looking man.

"I'd like that," I assured him. "But I don't have a glove."

"I'll buy you one," he told me.

I was ready to leave with him immediately.

Apparently all the paperwork had been done, because we were told to get our things. Except for the HOA clothes, we had no more luggage than when we arrived.

Edith said, "As we were leaving, Mrs. Keggie sneered at us."

"Who was Mrs. Keggie?" I asked.

"She was one of the matrons, and at one point you refused to go into the dining room because they were serving meat loaf.

So she slapped you, and I said, 'You slap my brother once more and I'll kick your behind.' So she said, 'Oh, you are some beauty. I wonder who's going to get you.'

"When we were leaving with Stella, Mrs. Keggie said, 'You've got a beauty there.' "

Alice nodded her head. "She was a nasty lady."

We took the subway to Penn Station and got on the Long Island Rail Road—an hour's journey to Hollis, in Queens.

The lady told us to call her Aunt Stella and the man said we could call him Harold.

On the train, she said, "I expect you children in bed by four o'clock." This was such a weird statement that I recently checked with my sister Edith and asked if she remembered Aunt Stella telling us that.

"Yes," she told me. "I also remember me saying to her, 'Morning or afternoon?' and she said, 'I'll tell you later.' "

It wasn't until years later that I discovered people took foster children into their homes to supplement their incomes. We were worth twenty-five dollars a month per child, and for many foster parents that paid the rent and the mortgage.

Once they realized that, foster children became very suspicious about why they had been placed in a particular home. We felt that if we were there for the support of their families, there was no sense becoming too friendly. But the Depression made people desperate. I never experienced any cruelty from the people I lived with, except when I was unhappy and invented it. So even if people were in it for the money, they were never unkind.

When we arrived in Hollis we were escorted into the living room, where Aunt Stella and Uncle Cyril's children were waiting for us. There was Harold, who had come with us; Ray, who had the best job in the family, selling fabrics to Broadway shows; Ira, who was a press agent; and Caroline, a secretary. They were all dressed nicely and greeted us warmly. No problem here, I thought to myself.

Aunt Stella said we would eat alone in the breakfast nook. That arrangement suited us fine because it meant that we wouldn't have to worry about table manners. The four of us agreed that things could be a lot worse.

We lucked out when we were sent to Hollis, because it was a very comfortable middle-class community. The streets were safe, and even people with little money kept up their lawns and gardens. The public schools were no more than a few blocks away, all the stores, except the A&P, had local ownership, and everyone seemed to know everyone else's business.

The Depression was all-consuming and many of the most affluent home owners were policemen, firemen, and civil servants because they all had safe jobs. People didn't bother to lock their doors. Yet times were tough for almost everybody. I remember banks closed and people standing out front hoping to get their money. Meat was served once a week in its original form, and then as meat loaf or hash.

Everything cost pennies, nickels, and dimes. For many families, paper money was a rare commodity. Aunt Stella's husband, Cyril, sold printed signs from store to store which said things like, "No Checks Cashed," "No Food Inside," "No Credit," "No Loitering."

Heads of households tried to make a living in any way they could. We would wait until evening to see how well Uncle Cyril had done during the day. If he was smiling, we knew he had sold some signs. If he had a pained expression on his face, we were aware that he had struck out. He had far more bad days than good days. People just couldn't afford signs.

According to the HOA's records, Uncle Cyril liked me very much, and I slept in Aunt Stella and Uncle Cyril's bedroom until the social worker told them to make other arrangements.

I was moved upstairs to the attic and shared a room with the Irish maid named Celeste. It turned out to be a very important event in my life.

Of all Aunt Stella's children, Harold was my favorite foster "cousin," because he used to slip me a dime when I ran down to the store for him. I ran errands for Ira, too—but he stiffed me.

Because I shared a room with the maid, I had an opportunity to observe her in all her glory. When she undressed or dressed, I always had one eye peeping over the cover. Her skin was the color of a light peach with freckles on it, and although I didn't have anything to compare them with, I somehow knew that she had the greatest breasts in the world.

The exact location of my bed was strategic for what went on very late at night. Harold used to come tiptoeing into the room and get on top of Celeste. At the time I thought Harold was hurting her because Celeste kept moaning and groaning. Later on as a freshman in high school, I found out that when a man and woman wrestled and moaned and grunted a lot, it did not necessarily mean they were mad at each other. It dawned on me that they had been screwing their brains out. When Harold came in to visit a consenting Celeste, I was the witness. I would watch them in wonder while they thrashed around, legs and hair flying, no more than five feet away—possibly closer.

Harold was my role model, and Celeste was the first woman I ever saw completely unclothed. Whatever they were doing had a lasting effect on me—the scene has stayed with me for many, many years, and I still seem to be attracted by women who look like Celeste.

When I told my sisters this story, after I started working on the book, Edith pursed her lips and said, "She was always a slut."

Alice agreed, and said, "Harold was never choosy."

Doris said, "You should have told the social worker."

I had no idea what she wanted me to tell her.

My real youth started in the Morais home. I lived there for about two years. It was a nice place and everyone treated me kindly. After a while, I just observed the family and absorbed everything that they said and did. Adults are very strange around children. They say and do things as if children don't exist, or have no eyes or ears. I became the invisible man.

It was also at this stage that I learned how to get people to like me. I found out that if I smiled at the person to whom I was talking, they became relaxed. I also learned that I could get what I wanted if I only showed enthusiasm.

During my stay at the Morais home, a boy named Michael Dolowitz came to live with us. He was from the HOA and he was what could be called a problem child. At nine or ten, Michael enjoyed setting fire to things, like the house. He got no pleasure from the blaze itself, but enjoyed seeing all the fire engines wheel up after he had pulled the alarm, and watching all the firemen go to work.

Michael also stole things and he made Aunt Stella's life an ordeal. I was his roommate, and I was fascinated about what he would do next.

One day, my tonsils swelled up, and I was in agony. While Aunt Stella was trying to deal with this problem, Michael pulled the fire alarm in front of the house, and three large fire trucks arrived on the scene. Aunt Stella alternated between talking to the fire chief and rushing upstairs to attend to me. The doctor finally arrived and swabbed my throat. I would not have remembered this incident if it hadn't coincided with the false alarm. I once asked Michael why he was always pulling the fire alarm, and he told me, "I like to get people mad." It made sense to me.

It wasn't long before they took Michael back to the HOA. I never heard what happened to him, though he is still a household word in our family. Maybe the asylum straightened him out. I sincerely hope so.

The one critical incident in my childhood that I have never forgotten took place on Red Brick Hill in Hollis on a bright, clear winter night. The ground was covered with snow and all the kids were laughing and shouting as they rode their sleds down the hill. I must have been seven or eight. I still remember how wonderful it all felt. The snow made everything glisten. I was feeling happy. I did not own a sled of my own, so I said to two boys standing next to me, "Can I borrow your sled?" One of them answered, "No." The other boy told him, "Let him have it. He doesn't have a mother."

Tears rolled down my cheeks as I rode down the hill on that borrowed sled. Those words have never left me. I wanted to yell that I did have a mother, but only a few people knew where she was and I was in no position to tell them. Sniffling quietly, I dragged the sled up the hill and gave it back.

I'm certain it was on that night on that hill that I vowed I would never ask anybody for anything again.

To this day, I'm just not very good at accepting gifts. Whenever I am given something, I become very embarrassed and uncomfortable. By the same token, I enjoy giving presents to other people. It's tough on everyone because no one can ever catch up with me.

Citizen Kane had his "Rosebud," and I had my "Red Brick Hill."

• • •

I finally did give that speech at the lunch celebrating the 150th anniversary of the HOA. Among the trophies now hanging on my wall, none compares with the plaque they gave me that day. It marks the scene of one of my greatest revenges.

The room was filled with New York's Jewish elite—the Our Crowd types, including the Lehmans, Guggenheims, Salomons, and Strausses. There were members of the Jewish Welfare Board, and those associated with the HOA before it closed. There were even social workers.

I felt the way General MacArthur must have felt when he came back to West Point. Of all the speeches I have given in my life, this was the most meaningful.

I told them how, somewhere in the dim past, when I was a foster child around ten years old, and I was fighting for my life, I dreamed that I would be the guest of honor at just such an affair. I didn't know the event would take place at the Pierre Hotel—I had never heard of the Pierre Hotel—but in my fantasy I saw myself at a podium such as this talking about the struggles of my childhood and how I had overcome them. In my fantasy, I even gave myself a standing ovation.

I then proceeded to set everyone straight on exactly where I fit into the Jewish child-care picture. It isn't easy to be a foster child, I said. You are in some sort of no man's land. If you lived in the HOA, you had the security of numbers. A foster home is something else again. The child knows instinctively that there is nothing permanent about the setup. At any time he or she can be swooped up and placed in another home.

The foster parents have a problem, as well. If they get too attached, they can be wounded if the child is suddenly taken away.

I must have been six or seven years old and terribly lonely and confused, when I said something like, "This stinks. I'm going to become a humorist."

From then on, I had one goal in mind and that was to make people laugh. I adopted the role of class clown. I made fun of authority figures, from the principal of the public school to the social worker who visited me every month. It was a dangerous profession I had chosen, because no one likes a funny kid. In fact, adults are scared silly of them and tend to warn children who act out that they are going to wind up in prison or worse.

It is only when you grow up that they pay you vast sums of money to make them laugh.

Performing for laughs was my salvation. The other thing that helped me escape the reality of our lives was to concoct mysterious stories about myself. I invented a mother and father and I made myself the only child. I had the usual dreams about being a great sports figure, one day Joe DiMaggio and Lou Gehrig the next. I dreamed that I was a movie star like Mickey Rooney, and a writer like Booth Tarkington. The lonelier I became, the more interesting I managed to make my dream world.

The best story I made up was that I was really the son of a Rothschild—a name that was revered in my foster home because they were so rich and so Jewish. I worked it out that I had been kidnapped by my nurse when I was six months old and sold to a couple named Buchwald who were going to America.

The Rothschilds had hired France's most famous detective to find me, and it was only a matter of time before he showed up on my doorstep in Hollis. Once my true identity was established, I would prevail on my real Rothschild father not to prosecute the people involved with my kidnapping.

But I did intend to disinherit Doris the next time she was mean to me.

All my life, the Hebrew Orphan Asylum has followed me in one way or another.

And then I told the audience a true story.

One evening, I attended a fancy dinner at the Tour d'Argent, the great temple of three-star dining in Paris. I was seated next to Doris Warner Leroy, the daughter of Harry Warner, one of the Warner Brothers.

We were chatting about this and that, and I turned to her and said, "Doris, you and I have something in common."

"What's that?" she asked.

"I was once in the Hebrew Orphan Asylum, and your father was one of its biggest supporters. He built the Warners' Gym, and we saw Warner Brothers films for free."

Doris went white. "Oh my God—no one has mentioned that place to me for twenty years. Oh my God."

"Well," I said, "don't get that shaken up by it. It had nothing to do with you."

Then she told me her story. It seems her father decided to show Doris how much better off she was than other children. So every Chanukah he made her get dressed in her fanciest outfit and go to the HOA and hand out gifts to the kids. They in turn spat on her.

She said, "I lived in dread of the HOA and it took me twenty years of analysis to forget it. Now we are in Paris and you have to bring that damn place up to me."

It was bizarre. Here we were, two people dining at the Tour d'Argent—both scarred by the same institution. She, because she had to hand out presents, and me because I had to accept them.

I ended my speech by saying, "As I look back on it, I owe a

great debt to the HOA, and to people such as yourselves who cared for the Jewish kids of New York City.

"I also want to thank you today for helping fulfill one of my best fantasies. I feel I had a unique experience as a child. Every once in a while, someone asks, 'How do you become a humorist?' I always reply, 'Well, first you have to become a foster child.' "

I got my standing ovation.

3

Life in Hollis

About this time, Aunt Stella was becoming disenchanted with all four of us. She was willing to keep my two older sisters, but she wanted to dump Doris and me. She said it had something to do with moving and she claimed that she would have no room in her new house for us.

Alice asked me, "How did you feel when you got the news?"

"I was pissed off. I felt we should have been kept together. We didn't have much as a family, but we had each other. Now they were going to break up the set." There wasn't anything I could do about it and no one I could protest to. Doris was delighted. She was sure the next home would be so much better. When they told me I was leaving I pretended it was a neat idea. No one realized that I was mad. I had dimples, which helped a lot. Not many people can get mad at a kid if he smiles all day long.

Leaving Alice and Edith behind at the Moraises', Doris and I left for a second foster home—yet another strange place in a short ten years of life. No matter where we went, the size of the bag we carried with us never changed. As they say on the tags of T-shirts—one size fits all.

On June 1, 1935, Doris and I arrived at the home of a family named Bergman, who lived only a few blocks away from Aunt Stella. The foster mother's name was Aunt Rae, and the foster father was Uncle Aaron, a German refugee tailor, who worked in the basement of the house repairing and pressing clothes, which I delivered. There were two other children living in the home, a brother and sister named Sol and Lillian Freid. Sol was a good-looking young boy. We were the same age, and we got along well because we shared the same enemies. Lorraine, for instance. She was the Bergmans' daughter, and she was very pretty, with long hair, pouting lips, and doe-like eyes. The four of us hated her. We thought she was stuck-up, and her mother showered all the good favors on her at our expense. We were convinced that we were being shortchanged.

From the start, there was friction. We didn't get along very well with "Aunt" and "Uncle," and they didn't get along very well with us. It was a question of authority. The four foster children refused to accept their foster parents' rules, and the apparent favoritism toward their own daughter was an added problem.

Sol, with whom I shared a room next to the kitchen, was angry that he had to go to Hebrew school after public school, and was in revolt. I don't remember what my particular problem was, but the social worker's records said, "Arthur has lost a good deal of animation and his easygoing nature since his placement in this foster home. It is obvious that the boy is not very happy in his present surroundings. At times the visitor has noticed an attitude of hostility between Arthur and foster mother. Arthur and his sister have become quarrelsome."

In spite of this, Doris continued to be very protective of me. I recall one incident around that time. I was wrestling on the grass with a boy called Buzzy Davis, when Doris rushed out of the house and yelled, "Stop hurting him."

Buzzy and I looked at each other, wondering what was going on.

"He wasn't hurting me," I said.

Doris responded, "Well, he better not."

When I mentioned this story to Doris, she had no memory of it at all. Even today the time spent in foster homes is too painful for her to recall. Doris was a very attractive child, and despite her troubles with her home life, she was popular in school and had many friends. She was smart and got good grades. She just can't stand to talk about our childhood.

In the daytime, Doris and I had a lot of freedom to wander, and we went everywhere in search of adventure. Sometimes we crashed motion picture houses by waiting at the side door for the movie to end and the audience to leave.

On occasion Doris and I would go into Jamaica and spend the ten cents' fare given to us on something to eat. Then at the signal from Doris, I would start crying and she would go up to a policeman and say that I had lost our bus fare. Almost always, he would dig into his pocket and give us a dime.

Sometimes I would stand in front of a bakery and cry very loudly with my nose pressed against the glass. Doris would say to someone, "He's very hungry—he hasn't eaten all day."

A kindly person would inevitably take us into the store.

Another entry showed up in the records that I don't recall: "Doris and Arthur complain about having to pay for articles of laundry which Mrs. Bergman has done up for them. Doris usually pays for this out of spending money the father gives her. Doris also says that she must do Arthur's shirts."

Mr. Bergman complained to the same worker that we were constantly disobeying him. He was right. Sol and I couldn't care less about him or Mrs. Bergman, so we pretended that they had no say over us.

There just was no meeting of the minds. It occurred to me later on in life that one of the things wrong with the setup was that there were two pairs of unrelated children, as well as a biological daughter whose parents took children in to supplement their income. We were definitely a dysfunctional foster family.

Chanukah was the toughest day of the year, because Lorraine was showered with gifts from her relatives, while we received a domino game or a paint set. This confirmed Doris' theory that Mrs. Bergman was making a fortune by starving us to death.

Doris was constantly thinking up ways of making us all envious. One of her tricks at meal time was to save her dessert, until everyone else had finished. Then she would take her fork or spoon and slowly eat the dessert while everyone watched. She did it in the Morais house and she did it in the Bergman house. I can still see her spooning her chocolate pudding and enjoying every moment of it. Saving her dessert for last was Doris' only way of asserting herself.

The Bergmans had a poodle and I took it out for a walk every night. As we strolled along, I would scare it by snapping the leash hard with a *crack* in front of him. I never hit him, but my voice was very cruel, and he shook in fear of me. I took out all my anger against the only one I could dominate—a harmless little dog. I have been so ashamed of this, I even debated whether to include it in this book or not.

Clearly, Mrs. Bergman was not happy with her charges, and we weren't overjoyed to be in her home, so Doris saw an opportunity to get us moved out. She told me to tell the social worker that we were being starved to death.

"The social worker will look at us and know it isn't true," I told her.

"Suck your cheeks in when you talk to her," Doris said.

By now I was beginning to understand the gist of being a foster child. If you didn't like a place, the person to see was the social worker, who did pay attention, since her main job was to oversee the welfare of the child. It would be nice to say that all the children's stories about the bad conditions of a particular foster home were true—but many were invented by the kids in hopes that the next home would be the one to fulfill their dreams.

In the case of the Bergmans, the worker had the word of the four of us. In the reports I've read, Mrs. Bergman felt that she wasn't appreciated by any of us and we were ungrateful. Everyone was right—but because her first responsibility was to the children, the social worker had to take our word over that of the foster parents.

Doris was on to this very early in the game, and she made the most of it.

The move from the Bergman household to the Devries home took place on February 2, 1936. The Devries family lived in what I considered a mansion on an eighth of an acre of land. It was located at number 90–12 196th Street, between Hillside and Jamaica Avenue. I only mention the address because I still remember it. The street was tree-lined and all the lawns were neatly trimmed.

Rose and Mike Devries were our new foster parents. Their sons were Carlton, twelve years old, and Leonard, who was thirteen. Doris and I were suspicious of both of them, though Carl never bothered us much. Leonard seemed hostile.

At a summit conference with Leonard and Carlton in Phoenix in 1992, where they had both retired, Leonard explained his reasons. "When I was a kid, I never liked you," he confessed. That took me aback, and I said, "How could anyone not like me?"

He replied, "Because you got new clothes twice a year and it really pissed me off."

That requires explanation. The HOA was my guardian all during my period as a foster child. It was responsible for my material welfare, and it supplied the social workers who visited us in Queens. It was also in charge of our medical well-being and our teeth. Many fillings in my mouth today were put there by students from the Columbia University Dental School.

Then there was our clothing. Twice a year we went into the home and were issued clothes. They were slightly old-fashioned, but they were new. My guess is that they were no longer selling and the manufacturers wanted to get rid of them.

Leonard's statement threw me because I never imagined that anyone would be jealous of the clothes I got from the HOA. I was very sensitive about such things. Once Mrs. Devries gave me ice skates that weren't new—hand-me-downs from Carl—but in perfectly good condition. I showed them to the boy who lived across the street, who sneered and said, "They're used." This hit me very hard, because it went deeper than the ice skates. Everything about me was hand-me-down, even the new clothes from the HOA. I never used the skates.

Leonard was continuing. "My mother took you and Doris in for money. We were broke and she needed the income from the Jewish Welfare Service. That really ticked me off. I was ashamed for my parents."

"I hadn't thought of you as being poor," I told him.

"At one time my father had a lot of money. He owned

wholesale meat lockers and was an acquaintance of Dutch Schultz. Then he became a land developer and was wiped out. We eventually lost the house on 196th Street to the bank."

I said, "I never knew any of this. How did your father get to know Dutch Schultz?" Schultz was a famous gangster.

He replied, "The way we heard it was that the Dutchman used to stash his money in my father's meat lockers. No one ever thought to look there. We heard that the Dutchman liked my father. Once my father was held up while carrying a paper bag of money and he told the Dutchman. The next day, it was returned in the same paper bag."

As in our previous foster homes, we called our new foster parents Aunt and Uncle and their children were "cousins." Every once in a while, someone smelled a rat and pressed us on our relationship to the foster parents, but we always managed to fudge it.

I am not sure why we were so frightened of being revealed as foster children. It might have been the connection with the words Hebrew Orphan Asylum. The last two words were heavy baggage for a child to carry. Now I revel in it. I guess there is a certain pride in being involved with an institution that even George Bush couldn't get into.

As with the other foster fathers before him, Uncle Mike left little impression on me. To this day, I can't imagine him hanging around with the likes of Dutch Schultz. He went out of the house at four in the morning, and when he came home he went straight to bed. We saw him on weekends. But I do remember that when there was a good show or a fight on the radio, Mike was there. It was the era of Max Schmeling, Joe Louis, Max Baer, and Primo Carnera. We gathered around the radio as close as we could get, cheering for the Jewish Max Baer to kick the shit out of the Nazi Max Schmeling. We also cheered for Joe Louis. I've seen a lot of fights on television and at ringside in my time, but none compared with listening to the great ones on radio.

One of America's favorite radio programs was Walter Winchell. He was a columnist who had power like no newspaperman ever had before or since. When he was on Sunday night in the spring and summer, every house blared out his staccato voice. If Walter didn't like Stalin, we didn't like him either. If a show or movie appealed to him, it was a surefire hit. He made J. Edgar Hoover a household name, and he was relentless with his enemies.

Years later I met Walter Winchell at the Roney Plaza—his hangout in Miami Beach. He seemed a bully and an egomaniac. He said to me, "Do you know what you young journalists owe to me?"

I took out a pad and pencil and said, "No, tell me."

He sensed that I planned to make him look foolish and he shut up.

What I wanted to say to him was, "You dumb SOB—you were part of my childhood."

The other great shows the family gathered in the living room to listen to were *One Man's Family, The Shadow, Amos and Andy,* Jack Benny, Fred Allen, and George Burns. I met Benny and Allen and George Burns and many other radio stars in Paris in the fifties, and the thrill was still there. Their voices were part of Hollis and will always remain with me.

Baseball was the big sport for my generation—and the Brooklyn Dodgers, New York Giants, and New York Yankees were the teams we rooted for.

Occasionally, the HOA got free tickets to the Yankee

games. Our heroes were Lou Gehrig and Joe DiMaggio. I was not a Yankee fan, but you didn't have to be one to love Joe DiMaggio. Just to see him play made you a very big man in our neighborhood. I never got close, but from the bleachers the HOA kids screamed their lungs out: "Joe, Joe, Joe."

The years went by—many, many years—and I was writing my column from Washington, D.C. One of my best friends was Edward Bennett Williams, the famed criminal lawyer. He was trying an SEC case in New York City. His client was Louis Wolfson, a wealthy entrepreneur, who was being accused of manipulating securities. Eddie and I had a date for lunch, and I went downtown to the Federal Court House to pick him up.

It was a jury trial and the courtroom was empty because it was the second time Wolfson was being tried—the first had ended in a hung jury, and the press couldn't care less.

I sat in the first row as the prosecutor questioned a witness. Suddenly the door opened in the back and in walked Joe DiMaggio. Everyone turned, including the jury.

Joe walked down the aisle and slid in next to me.

I was speechless. Here was the man I had worshiped all my childhood sitting next to me in living color. This was a few years before Simon and Garfunkel sang, "Where have you gone, Joe DiMaggio?" But when they did, they spoke for me.

Joe didn't even have to testify—all he had to do was shake hands with Lou and sit in the front row for a short while as the trial was in progress. Wolfson was found guilty—not even Joe DiMaggio could save him from that—but the impact was tremendous.

I've seen Joe DiMaggio since at Washington Redskins' football games and every time the magic never fades. I love him very much.

• • •

Aunt Rose made the deepest impression on me and it was a good one. She liked me. I know this because the records from the HOA say she did. I allowed myself to get close to her—but not too close because the world I was living in did not encourage emotional investment.

By this time, I had discovered that I could relate better to women than to men. My sisters played a big role in it, and so did my foster mothers. I never paid much attention to the foster fathers, and in all the homes the men were much weaker. I spent a good part of my childhood trying to please women.

For example, when I was ten and living at the Bergman home, I used to hang out at the place of a neighbor who lived three houses down. She liked me, and so I ran errands for her. I even helped sort out her laundry. Mrs. Bergman was jealous of the time I spent there, particularly since I did things for this lady I did not do for her.

Almost every woman I have ever known has been some kind of surrogate mother to me. I'll do anything for their approval. I cherish them, I worship them, I like to listen to them, and I flirt with them.

I have a different relationship with men. I get along nicely with them, unless they try to harm me or somebody else. I'm a good listener and I keep secrets, but I enjoy the company of women a lot more.

The Devries family home had a pleasant atmosphere and a lovely sunny porch. Except for not having a real live-in mother and father, it was as good as you could get.

There was also Aunt Rose's extended family—sisters and brothers and in-laws who, on the whole, were very nice to me. I even edited a newspaper which I called "The Family Gossip." It was handprinted and revealed all the hot news in the family.

One of my favorite satirical targets was Uncle Walter, Aunt Rose's happy-go-lucky brother-in-law who was an insurance agent. Uncle Walter worked for the Prudential Life Insurance Company and there wasn't anyone he wouldn't sell a policy to. He even sold me one, for twenty-five cents a week, which I paid on for several years. I never collected on it, so I figured out the other day that Prudential owed me $25,000,000.

In "The Family Gossip," I also accused Uncle Walter of shortchanging me on washing his car. I printed one copy and passed it around at family gatherings, waiting for laughter and compliments. Things haven't changed much. I'm still doing the same thing—showing my writing to others and waiting for a reaction.

Aunt Ruth, Aunt Pauline, and Aunt Augusta were all related. They accepted me as part of the family. I never felt treated as an outsider.

People tell me that I was a sloppy dresser. My socks were constantly falling down and my shirttail was always sticking out. Throughout my childhood, everyone in charge of me asked the same question, "Did you brush your teeth?"

A few years ago, I went back to 196th Street when *Newsday* did a story about me. I went with my childhood friends Audrey and Jack Mindermann. The house where I had lived now had siding on it—which I hated. There was a small front yard, which I am sure was far bigger in the old days, and a screen porch which also was smaller than I remembered it. The entire neighborhood had shrunk since I left.

I had lived in the front room on the second floor overlooking the street. I longed to see it. So I rang the bell. A black woman answered the door and opened it just wide enough for four tiny heads to pop out. She and the children were suspicious of me.

I said, "Hi. I used to live here and I was wondering if I could visit the room where I grew up?" The woman and all four children shook their heads "no" at the same time. And slammed the door.

That taught me a lesson. If you are going to visit the scenes of your childhood, don't bring the press and a photographer with you.

During the return visit to Hollis, I put on a pair of roller skates to show off on the paved schoolyard of P.S. 35. It took fifteen minutes before it all came back, and suddenly I was doing figure eights and skating just like ice skating champ Dick Button. I was doing fine, when one of two kids watching yelled, "Atta boy, Grandpa." That hurt.

Hollis was more or less the place I lived the longest in my youth, and I considered it my own hometown.

It wasn't Beverly Hills, but it had clean streets and warm smells. A block down from the theater was the public library. That was my home away from home. Books were my escape. I traveled to far-off continents, dove underneath oceans, and visited outer space long before it became fashionable. I read Booth Tarkington and Mark Twain, Gene Fowler, Damon Runyon, and, when I found out it was pornography, Voltaire's *Candide.* To this day, I love libraries—and I revere books. No matter how lousy the book, I don't have the heart to throw one away.

P.S. 35 was the hub of life when I lived at the Devries home. I remember all my teachers. The most ferocious was tiny Mrs. Dunlap, who taught music. I didn't like her, because I couldn't carry a tune. Once she was organizing *The Chimes of Normandy,* an operetta, for our class, and since I couldn't sing, I asked her, "Why can't we have a play?" She looked at me with daggers in her eyes and said, "You Bolshevik."

During my life I've been called a Communist many times, but Mrs. Dunlap was the only one who ever accused me of being a Bolshevik.

P.S. 35 has a cannon that honors General Nathaniel Woodhull, who was a Revolutionary War hero and fought Redcoats in the neighborhood. My friend Jack Mindermann thought he would have some fun one day, so he went to the principal, Mrs. Post, and told her that his father had found out the cannon was pointing in the wrong direction. The British had attacked from the other side—the west, not the east. He drove her crazy when he said that his parents were going to inform the newspapers that P.S. 35 had a cannon that was poised to fire on our own boys.

One of my most vivid memories of P.S. 35 is of a bully named Sam Morelli. Sam looked like a gorilla and attended a parochial school called St. Gerard's. He got out earlier in the afternoon, in time to wait for me by the P.S. 35 playground gate.

This is how the dialogue went:

Sam: "Hey, Jew."

Me: "Yes sir."

Then he would smack me on the nose and it would start to bleed. This went on for some time—at least until Sam graduated and went off to Catholic high school.

The years went by and I had forgotten much of the trauma of my youth when a little old couple came into the city room of the *Paris Herald Tribune.*

"We're Sam Morelli's parents," they said. "And he told us

that if we got to Paris to be sure and look you up. He still talks about the wonderful times you used to have when you were kids in Hollis."

I swear my nose started to bleed again.

As a professional funny man, I raised particular hell in my English class, where I drove Mrs. Egorkin crazy. English turned out to be my best subject. Every Thursday we had the equivalent of "show and tell." Each child was supposed to perform, read, sing, or talk about a worm they had found in the garden.

I loved Thursdays and I prepared all week for one-man plays which poked fun at everyone. To give you some idea of how much recognition I was yearning for, I stood in front of my class and announced, "*Deirdre's Bloomers,* produced and directed by Art Buchwald. Written by Art Buchwald and starring Art Buchwald."

The show went like this: There was a girl in class named Deirdre who was very snobbish, and I made her the butt of my act. I said, "We are about to begin the show, but where is Deirdre?"

I replied in another voice, "Deirdre has special bloomers—they are so tight that she has to keep her nose up in the air." (Much laughter).

I used falsetto when I had Deirdre talking to her mother. "Mother, do you think I am stuck-up?"

"Of course not. When you stick your nose in the air, you can smell better."

The roar of my classmates was the most beautiful sound I had ever heard. Not only did I love the moments, but I sensed when they were coming. I didn't know what the word "comedian" meant, but Mrs. Egorkin had made me one. Who needed parents when you could make people laugh?

One time in "show and tell," I recited a poem I had written called "The Lone Cowboy." It went:

With a pack on my back and a snack in my pack,
I'll roam the lone prairie.
And I'll yodel all day and I'll sleep through the night
and I'll be a cowboy free.
And I'll talk to my hoss as he rolls and tosses,
far from the corral he'll be.
Down the ravine and over the hill, across the plains,
it's really a thrill—and it's the life for me.
With a pack on my back and a snack in my pack,
I'll roam the lone prairie,
And I'll yodel all day and I'll sleep through the night
and I'll be a cowboy free.

I worked very hard on this and I was very proud of it. But Mrs. Egorkin thought that I had lifted it from a book and she implied that I hadn't written it. Nothing in my youth, except possibly the incident on Red Brick Hill, could have hurt more. I bit my lips so that I wouldn't cry. I also refused to respond to her grilling. A few days later, Mrs. Egorkin realized that she was wrong, on two counts: one, by questioning me about the authorship of the poem, and two, by humiliating me in front of the class. She apologized publicly, and after that she was very supportive of everything I wrote. The end of this story is that Mrs. Egorkin became an important influence in my life, and we kept up with each other until she died. We even appeared on a television quiz show together.

If a child is lucky, there will always be one Mrs. Egorkin who'll play a pivotal role in his or her life.

Many moons later, I became involved in a suit against Paramount Pictures over a film called *Coming to America*, which starred Eddie Murphy. I sued them for stealing my idea for the picture. In the course of the trial, one of Paramount's lawyers tried to prove that I had never written the treatment for the film, and that I had stolen it from Charlie Chaplin's movie *A King in New York*. It was one of a long series of studio cheap shots.

But it hit me the same way Mrs. Egorkin's accusation about "The Lone Cowboy" poem hit me. The idea of being accused of stealing another person's literary property ranks in my mind with committing a felony.

The judge threw out the Paramount accusation and said that the Chaplin movie bore no resemblance to my story. But while it was up in the air and the accusation of plagiarism went round the world on the wire service, I seriously—and I do mean seriously—concluded that if the charges stuck for any reason, I didn't want to live.

Paramount, of course, knew nothing about "The Lone Cowboy." They were unaware that the seeds of my lawsuit had been planted in Mrs. Egorkin's "show and tell" class, and that I would do anything to prevent the theft of my literary property.

P.S. 35 was my first showcase for humor. I have often wondered whether, if I had had a different childhood, I would still have become a humorist. I'm not certain. I might have been funny, but except for the folks at the Aetna Curtain Company no one would have known it.

Laughter was the weapon I used for survival. All my life I have been able to sense a person's weak spot. I use humor as a way to insult. I hate junk telephone calls, for instance, and one day, I got a call at the office from a person claiming to work for Shearson American Express. He wanted to know who was handling my investments. I told him that it was none of his business. He said, "Well, I could handle them better." I exploded. "How come if you're sitting in a basement in front of a bank of phones making five dollars an hour, you can invest my money better than I can?"

My anger was buried deep behind the humor. I have always had trouble with anger. I have swallowed it, and it's come back later to give me the shakes. As a child, I vowed never to show it, no matter how upset I became—because if I did, everybody would discover that I wasn't a nice person. My heroes in this world are those who can get rid of their anger and not feel bad about it.

People ask what I am really trying to do with humor. The answer is, "I'm getting even." I am constantly avenging hurts from the past. Speaking to the HOA at its 150th anniversary was one example. I have also addressed large gatherings of Marine officers—active and retired—and that has always been a wonderful way of making up for any bad experiences I had in the Marines. For me being funny is the best revenge.

Writing humor in my column isn't as dangerous as performing it. If I fail in front of a live audience, the humiliation is as great as anything a human being can suffer. When I'm standing on a stage or on a dais, there is no second chance. I know that I damn well better be funny the first time or they'll send me back to the quarantine ward at the HOA.

As a kid, I often traveled from Hollis to the neighboring town of Jamaica, and it was there that I almost became involved in a life of crime. I was eleven years old and I dropped in to visit Woolworth's. I had a dime in my pocket and as I wandered around the store, I stopped to examine a small tin bank, the size of a sardine can. I picked it up and was ready to pay for it, but no one was around to wait on me, so I stuck it under my shirt and headed for the door. As I stepped out on the sidewalk, an arm came down heavily on my shoulder and a giant of a man wearing a fedora and chewing on a cigar said, "Whatcha got under your shirt?"

I cried, "I'll pay for it."

He grabbed my arm and dragged me to the office in the rear of the store. I was surrounded by the manager, a clerk, and a store policeman. I did the only thing I could under the circumstances—I cried. I held out the dime as an offering to Woolworth's.

The manager gave me a lecture on shoplifting. "That's how John Dillinger started out," he yelled at me. "He stole banks from five-and-dimes."

The lady in the office said, "I am glad I am not your mother." And the store dick said, "We're wasting our time—let's call the G-men."

Finally it was decided to let me go—on condition that I never enter the store again. Over sixty years have gone by, and to this day I have kept the promise and have never gone into a Woolworth's store.

It wasn't a bad lesson. They did scare the hell out of me. If the incident hadn't taken place, I might have wound up in the underworld or at least in the public relations business. I have been involved in other petty crime, but the big stuff I left to Willie Sutton and Ivan Boesky.

Hollis was a small town and Jamaica was a big one. In the golden age of my youth, Jamaica had six movie theaters. There was the Carlton, featuring live entertainment; the Loew's Valencia; across the street was the Alden; and down the block were the Merrick, the Savoy, and the Hillside. The Valencia was the St. Patrick's Cathedral of movie theaters. It had a live organist and was decorated by the same person who had designed the *Arabian Nights.* It has sentimental value for me, because the first photo of me to appear in a newspaper was taken there. There was some local event at the Valencia, and the photographer was shooting pictures of the dignitaries, when I slipped in and posed with them. The caption under the photo in the *Long Island Press* identified all the people, and at the end read, "Arthur Buchwald of Hollis, who had to prove to his mother he saw the movie."

The Carlton was on Jamaica Avenue and many famous orchestras appeared there. I took Sammy Kaye's girl home from there when I was twelve years old. Kaye was a very famous orchestra leader, and his slogan on the radio was "Swing and Sway with Sammy Kaye."

There was a stage door where all the fans hung out. Parked in front of the door was Sammy's Lincoln convertible, and sitting in it was one of the most beautiful girls in the world—Sammy's date. We stood around talking to her for more than an hour. She kept looking at her watch and finally she had had it. She turned to us and said, "Who wants to walk me home?" Four of us yelled, "I will."

It turned out she lived in Queens Village, and we surrounded her like the Praetorian Guard. After six blocks, Sammy Kaye pulled alongside the curb and yelled to "our girl" that he was sorry. He told her to get in the car, and damned if she didn't. I wasn't bitter. As they drove off, I thought, "At least we had her for a little while."

We went to the Hollis Theater on Saturday afternoons and

sat behind girls and pulled their hair—they would scream—but they also screamed if we didn't. The first show started around one o'clock. Many of the kids stayed right through the second show and the third. About six o'clock, a parade of parents with the ushers shining flashlights marched up and down the aisle looking for their little darlings. When a child was found, they were yanked by the collar or the hair toward the exit while the survivors sank deeper into their seats.

They also gave out gifts if you came for the serials. They were piled on the stage, and our ticket stub was our lottery number.

I won a chemistry set once. I wish I could say that this generated an interest in science, but it didn't. I have flunked every chemistry test I have ever taken.

Our hangout in Hollis was a candy story named Cerut's. I received my sex education there. Most everything I know about the birds and bees, I learned at the soda fountain. Things like:

> "If you stick your tongue in a girl's mouth, she will automatically have a baby."
>
> "If you neck in the back seat of a car, you have a much better chance of penetrating a woman than if you sit in the front seat."
>
> And "If you play with yourself for too long, you will go insane."

Most of us were prepared to be taken off to the booby hatch at any moment.

We had thirteen-year-old instructors who knew everything

there was to know about sex. The scary thing about our education was that when we turned thirteen, we became the instructors.

We had a big break once. My youth was spent on 196th Street. Down the street, we played tackle football in a lot, and the ground was as hard as cement. We had no equipment whatsoever, but for some reason, kids did not get hurt. Next to the field was a concrete revetment, the ruins of townhouses that were never built. One Saturday we showed up to play—twelve- and thirteen-year-olds—and, lo and behold, in the revetment someone had dumped a ton of illustrative pornography, all of it illustrated. I'm not exaggerating. Either the vice squad or gentlemen in the business had dumped all the dirty pictures there—and I mean they were dirty. We dove in as if it were a heated swimming pool, stuffing as many photos under our shirts and pants as we could handle. There was no football *that* day. At lunch time, we tried to sneak our booty into the house—but several of us were caught and were made to tell all. Lunch was canceled, as a steaming delegation of parents marched down to the revetment and stared in disbelief. The police were called, and as we stood across the street giggling, more police arrived, and finally officers with gold braids all over their uniforms and hats. They decided that it was too difficult to cart the porno stuff away, and the only thing to do was to burn it.

But they didn't burn everything. We managed to smuggle enough photographs to our rooms to satisfy our curiosity. We used them frequently to achieve instant gratification.

Most such self-abuse took place either in bed or behind the railroad tracks. My partner in crime was my foster cousin, Milton Stevens. We used to buy a pack of Kools, the mentholated cigarette, which we hid in a can. Then after school we would go to our hideaway and smoke a cigarette or two and then turn our backs on each other and seek nirvana. We found smoking and then flailing away an excellent after-school pastime.

To show you how different people remember things, Milton insists that we smoked Camels.

The last time I saw him I argued that Camels had no menthol taste, and we always wanted menthol to go with what we were going to do afterward.

One of the highlights of being part of the Hebrew Orphan Asylum was summer camp. The HOA ran its own boys' camp at Bear Mountain, New York (there was also one for the girls), called Camp Wakitan, and both the boys in the institution and the foster children were permitted to attend for a month.

The camp was located on a beautiful lake, and it was well run by a man named Pop Sprung, who was our own Father Flanagan. He was a lawyer and his big moment came when he prosecuted Japanese war criminals after World War II. Once out of the Army, he specialized in representing Japanese businessmen. We used to kid him that he was the only lawyer we knew who, if he couldn't get a war criminal hanged, worked for him on retainer.

I wasn't satisfied just to swing through the trees. I worked for the camp doctor, which gave me special privileges and some authority over the other campers. I needed that, because the camp was divided between the HOA boys and the foster children. The HOA boys didn't like foster kids and thought we were snobs. They ran in packs—the foster kids ran alone. My medical job saved me a great deal of woe. It was the equivalent of a painted red cross on my forehead.

It was in camp that I also learned to play chess. I didn't know it at the time, but it turned out to be one of the most useful skills I have acquired. Being able to play chess has helped me through many a bad period, and when I was with the Marines in the Pacific, it also helped me to pass the time when we had nothing else to do.

I asked my cousin Eddie if he remembered anything about our camp days, since we shared the same cabin.

He said, "I recall once taking your comb, and when you asked for it back, I combed my pubic hair."

I told him, "That's a hell of a note—did you ever ask God to forgive you?"

He replied, "Should I have?"

Camp life wasn't a completely happy experience for me. We were on this lake, and there was an Episcopalian camp down the road. As luck would have it, two kids I played with in Hollis went to this camp. All the time I attended Wakitan, I lived in deathly fear that they would see me and find out that I was connected with the Hebrew Orphan Asylum. So every time I thought I saw Harry Bischoff or Frank Davis from the Hollis neighborhood, I ducked behind a tree. I'm sure I would have had a better time if the fear factor hadn't played such an important part in my summer experience.

At a P.S. 35 reunion years later, I told both Davis and Bischoff how they had ruined my summers. Frank said, "Hell, we weren't even looking for you."

One of my major dreams when I was a kid was to return to Hollis as a conquering hero. I imagined going back as grand marshal of a spectacular parade like the Macy's Thanksgiving Day affair. In my mind I created floats depicting different stages of my life. I saw myself in a white convertible escorted by the American Legion Band and Knights of Columbus. I also imagined a ticker tape parade, even though there wasn't a building on Jamaica Avenue over two stories high. I decided that it was the least the Hollis leaders could do to acknowledge the recognition I had brought to the town.

I had to wait almost thirty years, but the invitation to come back finally arrived, not from the town fathers but from a small Unitarian church on Hillside Avenue. The minister asked me to give a talk. It wasn't the hero's welcome I had yearned for as a child, but I grabbed it before he changed his mind.

I called the Carey Limousine company and told them I wanted to hire the longest limo in New York. I intended to return in style.

Now this is the sad part of the story. The day I was scheduled to go out there, New York had a terrible ice storm and I received a call from the limo company that afternoon telling me it was too dangerous to send their driver to Queens.

I was upset and said, "What the hell am I going to do?"

The lady replied, "Take the subway like everybody else." I learned a new truth: you can't go home again—at least not by Carey Limousine.

New York Governor Mario Cuomo came from Hollis, too. I didn't know him when I was there, but it turned out that we both went to P.S. 35. One time at a lunch at the Waldorf Astoria, I was sitting next to him on the dais, and I mentioned that I had gone to the same school as he had. He immediately reacted and said, "Did you ever have Mrs. Laub for arithmetic?"

"Of course I did. What about Mrs. Gomez?" I asked. "I'll never forget her," he said. Now the amusing part is that every time we mentioned a teacher, both of us were waving our arms about. Out in the audience were fifteen hundred of New York's leading citizens who thought we were having a helluva fight. When the lunch was over, a friend who was in the audience came up and said, "What were you and Cuomo ready to kill each other about?"

"Nothing," I replied. "We were just comparing teachers at P.S. 35."

Four months later, I saw the governor and said, "I have bad news for you. Guess who else grew up in Hollis?"

"Who?" he asked.

"Elliott Abrams."

The governor said, "Damn."

At that time, Abrams was in charge of our Central American policy under Reagan and was the extreme right's fair-haired boy.

All my childhood triumphs were solo. I once roller-skated from Hollis to New York on Queens Boulevard. I could not have been more than ten years old. I even crossed the Queensborough Bridge on skates. Late that afternoon I showed up at Franklin Simon, a department store on Fifth Avenue where my sister Edith worked. She was horrified and gave me subway fare to return home. I was exhilarated with my accomplishment. The only thing I was able to compare it with was Lindbergh crossing the Atlantic. And like Lindbergh, I found a whole new world across the bridge there in Manhattan.

4

New York City Adventures

Let me tell you about my second life—the one I led in New York City while spending time as a foster child in Queens.

My father worked out of a loft on 23rd Street and Seventh Avenue. It was a third-floor walk-up, large and dark, and the main piece of furniture was a long table on which he could stretch out his drapes and curtains. Many nights he slept on the table rather than go home to his room in the Bronx.

I enjoyed being there because it was usually just Pop, myself, and his seamstress. I watched him work with fascination. He kept tacks in his mouth when he talked to me, and it made me very nervous.

It was the sight of the tacks in his mouth that convinced me to have no part of the curtain business.

I don't remember much about our conversations. My father used the word "dasn't" a lot. "You 'dasn't' do this" and "You 'dasn't' do that." We never got down to our personal lives too much, but skated around all the subjects that a child might want to explore with his father.

For as long as I can remember the word handed down from my sisters was, "Don't worry Papa, he has too much on his mind as it is." So I never worried Pop, and I never got to know him.

As I think back on it, the rule in the family was never to worry anybody else about anything. Even today most of our conversations start like this, "Don't tell Alice and Edith . . ." or, "Don't tell Arthur and Doris, but . . ." We were always a family that kept things under the carpet, and we still do.

I spent many Saturdays in my father's place. Two things stand out about it. One was that the seamstress, Rhoda, was beautiful and blonde. The other was that sewing curtains and slipcovers was not her only profession. She was also a call girl. One of the reasons she worked for my father was so she'd have a telephone available for her customers to call her for an appointment. The phone never stopped ringing.

I didn't know what was going on at the time, but years later, my father told me about it. Rhoda was a very hard worker and did not demand high wages, because the phone was more important to her than the salary he paid her. She was very pleasant, and since she practiced her second profession after hours it didn't appear to bother my father at all. At the same time, he refused to take messages for her, as he felt this would make him an accomplice in her moonlighting job. Uncle Oscar once told me, "She had the best of both worlds. It was curtains in the daytime and drapes at night."

I got along with her very well. Rhoda was a good listener and was particularly interested in knowing if I had any love life. I didn't, since I was twelve at the time.

She assured me that it wouldn't be long before I became

involved with a girl. This interested me, and I asked her what I was supposed to do.

"Treat her with respect," she said. "Women need men, but they don't want them if the men just want sex. Be careful if you make love with them that they don't have a baby."

"How can I stop it?" I asked.

"You should wear a rubber so your jism can't hit her egg."

"You mean if my white stuff gets to her egg, she will have a baby?"

"The chances are excellent that this could happen. You have to be careful because if you make her pregnant when you're very young you'll make a mess of your life and hers. Once you're married, then it's time for you to have babies."

Now this was the kind of stuff my father should have been telling me, but he didn't—so I heard it from a seamstress named Rhoda and I took her advice from then on.

Besides the call girl, there was another fascinating character in the loft, a Mr. Frisch. He was an inventor, and he worked in a makeshift lab in the back of the loft. He had a very interesting project. Frisch was trying to develop a coffee bag which looked like a tea bag. He hoped to come up with something so that you could make your own cup of coffee by dipping the bag in hot water. This was before instant coffee. My father had a piece of the action, because Mr. Frisch could not afford to pay any rent. Our entire family dreamed of Frisch hitting it big, but it was not to be. He was unable to make coffee behave like tea, and just when we thought there might be a breakthrough, he ran out of cheesecloth.

On the second floor of my father's building was a run-down Chinese restaurant. Pop had an arrangement with the management of the place to give me any food I wanted and he would pay for it when he saw them. My favorite dish was fried rice.

They made it nice and greasy with lots of pork and very little shrimp. It also had scallions, a scrambled egg, and God knows what else. The place was empty on Saturdays, so I asked to sit by the window overlooking Seventh Avenue. I behaved very grownup. When the waiter came over I studied the dirty menu, pretending that I couldn't make up my mind, and finally I would say, "How is the fried rice?"

The waiter always played the game. "Best in the house," he'd say.

"Then I'll have some."

I never wavered from the fried rice and they never wavered from saying, "Best in the house."

The memory of the restaurant is a very pleasant one for me. When I go to a Chinese establishment today I order fried rice, although it's never greasy enough for my taste.

One of my father's best business deals was with a men's clothing manufacturer named Mr. Seltzer. They had a barter arrangement—curtains for clothes. Mrs. Seltzer ordered what she needed for her living room windows, and Pop and I got a couple of suits off the racks of Seltzer's factory. The suit racks stretched out for miles, and I thought to myself: Seltzer must be richer than Rothschild. When my father took me there (it had to have been during the week because no one on Seventh Avenue worked on Saturdays), Mr. Seltzer waited on me himself—squeezing my cheeks and telling my father what a nice boy I was. Although there were thousands of suits I was never able to choose one myself, because Seltzer always selected ones that were just "right" for me.

If I mentioned that I didn't like a particular style, Pop would say, "Seltzer knows best or he would not have this business."

I haven't forgotten Seltzer. Whenever I buy a suit, my mind

goes back to that fabulous factory and I wish he were still around—and if he were, I wonder if he would make a barter deal with me.

My writing career began in my father's loft. He had a typewriter. I was about ten or eleven and I decided to write a book. It was about a boy born to a very rich family in France who was kidnapped at birth by a terrible nanny and brought to the United States, where he was sold to a family who lived in Hollis. He had three wicked daughters named Alice, Edith, and Doris. The French family finally found the boy and put the nanny in jail and sent the three wicked daughters to pick cotton in the South.

I wasn't just writing this book for amusement. I had seen an ad in the newspaper about a children's story contest, and the price was one thousand dollars. I was determined to win, so I wrote chapter one, over a period of four Saturdays, and when I finished I walked from Seventh Avenue to lower Park Avenue and took the elevator up to the publisher.

I asked to see the person in charge of the contest, and a woman appeared, with a pencil in her hair. I told her that I had written the first chapter of my book, which I had with me. Instead of throwing me out, she took me in to meet all the other editors, who surrounded me as I described my story with great gusto. Then someone kindly said, "This isn't really a contest for children, although there's no reason why a child couldn't write a book, and we would be very happy to read it when you have finished." Everybody was trying to keep a straight face. But I walked out very proudly and went back to my father's loft to continue. If they had not been nice people, they could have cut my writing career short. Today I hear from many young writers wanting to break in to the business. I am very responsive and always write to them. I do this because I think of that small group of editors who took the time to be nice to me long, long ago.

New York was the glamorous town that you only see now in old movies and on Broadway stages. The sky was lit up with dancing neon signs. It was safe to walk out in the streets. You were expected to show respect for the police. If you watched and listened, you got the greatest education that money couldn't buy.

I was only thirteen, but it was no problem to move around. People physically fought without noticing me; bookies took bets and every hotel lobby had a chair especially reserved for me.

My New York trips cost a nickel on the subway, and they were my introduction to the world I intended to join as soon as I finished school. It gave me an opportunity to study people and put them in pigeonholes. It was an education that did so much more for me than anything I could learn in school.

Besides going to my father's place, I walked around the city, running into one bizarre situation after another. One time I went into a coffee shop off Broadway. Every man in the place was wearing a wide-brimmed hat. I was sitting on a stool, when four gentlemen to my right dressed in zoot suits started to yell at two gentlemen on my left.

"Anyone from New York is an asshole."

The gentleman on my left retorted, "The only place where there are real assholes is Detroit. Let me make one phone call and we'll break your big thick heads against the counter." The discussion continued along the lines as to who would cause the most bodily damage.

At that moment, the New York thugs were outnumbered, but they claimed it didn't matter. "We'll shove these stools down your throats."

"Says who?" growled a zoot suit from Michigan.

I was in the middle, watching the argument as if it were a tennis match. Then one of the men from Detroit threw a sugar bowl past my head, missing the New York thug by inches. The man from New York took a blackjack out of his pants, and said, "You better get out of here, kid," which made sense to me.

I stood outside on the street watching the battle inside, until the cops came. Later on when I became a fan of Damon Runyon's, I knew better than most people what he was talking about. I did look in the newspaper the next day to see how many people in wide-brimmed hats had been killed in coffee shops off Broadway. There was nothing in the *Daily Mirror* about anybody being found with a stool up his ass. I knew I should have called in the story and offered an eyewitness account.

Another activity in New York on Saturdays was to go down to the Biltmore Hotel and stare at all the college girls who were being picked up by their Ivy League dates. In the golden age of American coeds, the girls dressed in suits, cashmere sweaters, silk blouses, silk stockings, and high heels.

I fell in love with every one of them.

I used to pretend that I was a college student. I bought a can of Prince Albert tobacco and a forty-nine-cent pipe with money I made delivering flowers. I would sit in the lobby, puffing on my pipe and pretending that I was Joe College waiting for my own date. I did this until I got dizzy and sick to my stomach. Then I would make a dash for the men's room. After upchucking for all I was worth, I went back to my chair and refilled the pipe. My hope at that moment was that some silk-stockinged, high-heeled coed would get into a fight with her date and come over to me and say, "I've had it with this jerk from Yale. Take me to the Stork Club—I'll pay."

I revealed my fantasy many years later when I spoke at a

Vassar commencement. After the speech, several women came up to me and said things like, "We should have taken you to the Stork Club."

The first Broadway play I ever saw was a Saturday matinee of *Tobacco Road.* Some people considered it obscene because Will Geer peed on the stage. I sat in the second balcony for fifty-five cents. From my vantage point, I could see down on the stage. Will didn't actually pee—he just pretended to—so I didn't know what all the fuss was about.

I owned New York. I visited every part of Manhattan. I rode the Staten Island Ferry back and forth for five cents. If you went early enough, the big theaters such as the Paramount, Strand, and Palace had special low prices. They also had truant officers stationed inside to nab the kids who were cutting school. And then there was 42nd Street, which featured dirty movies. I frequented them, as well as Minsky's live burlesque shows. The posters on the outside promised a lot more than what was going on inside.

In 1969, when I wrote my play *Sheep on the Runway,* the rehearsal hall was on 42nd Street in the same theater I attended as a boy. It was good to be back, but like everything else, even with the bright lights it seemed so much smaller. Minsky's was gone, and the dirty films being shown looked much sleazier than in the old days—or was it the people in the audience?

In the spring and the fall I loved to wander in Central Park on Sunday afternoons. I spent my time watching girls and boys doing what they did best in the park—holding hands and each other on park benches and whispering secrets. As well as the theaters, I also liked to go to the Museum of Natural History.

I rode the double-decker Fifth Avenue buses from Manhattan all the way up to Fort Tryon Park. I wasn't afraid to go anywhere or meet anybody. Many times, I initiated conversations with strangers. I always added two or three years to my age so that people would think more of me.

I would stop in the park and say, "That's a nice baby you've got there. What's his name?"

"George."

"I have a baby brother like that at home. He cries all night." (Lies, all lies.)

"Where do you live?"

"In Hollis, New York, but my family comes from France. I have a wicked nanny, but she doesn't know where I am."

And so it went—with every weekend I grew increasingly bold and street wise.

I had little money when I was a child. But I had enough. I worked all the time. When I was eight or nine, I sold magazines. I peddled the *Saturday Evening Post* and *Country Home Gentlemen.* I also sold *Colliers* and the *Ladies' Home Companion.* The way they induced boys to sell the magazines was to show them a very slick catalogue filled with bikes, scooters, and pinball machines. We earned points for the number of magazines sold. I went from door to door, not to earn money but to win a scooter. I did pretty well, and years later, after I saw *Death of a Salesman* on the stage, I identified with Willy Loman. We both knew what it was like out there.

I also caddied when I was thirteen. A golf course called Fresh Meadows was near us, and they were short of caddies on weekends so I went out there and waited to be sent on a round. What I usually got was one or two women who the regular caddies wanted no part of. Sometimes I carried two bags and the going was very, very slow. The women talked a lot and kept putting on lipstick. When they lost a ball, they refused to continue until I found it. If I couldn't, they weren't nice to me. I got even by looking up their dresses when they were bent over for a shot.

The caddying experience affected my life, because I vowed if I ever grew up and could afford it, I would never have anything to do with golf again. I have kept the promise to this day. The game made no sense to me when I was a kid and it makes no sense to me now. By not playing golf, I save hours of time to do what I want to do, and to enjoy myself.

I also worked for a florist in Jamaica as a delivery boy. The shop was owned by a Greek man named Dan Markellos. I couldn't have earned more than a dollar a day, but it was an introduction into the big time. I got to talk to everyone—customers, passersby, and Mr. Markellos, who was a gentle man and taught me to love roses. Delivering flowers is an emotional experience, because your appearance usually symbolizes a happy occasion—an anniversary, a birthday, a gesture of love and friendship. The person receiving the flowers is surprised and flattered, and therefore the tips are better than if you were delivering calves' liver or cleaning fluid.

In all my time as a floral delivery boy, I never met anyone who got mad at me for standing at the front door holding a box of roses in my hand.

I invested most of my profits in eclairs, cream puffs, and Napoleons. I think I've been investing in pastries all my life.

After Markellos, I got a job delivering flowers for Kottmiller's, a society florist in New York at the Hotel Roosevelt. My deliveries took me all over—from the fancy estates of Westchester to the magnificent apartments on Park Avenue. It was during the Depression, but the rich were even richer then, and some of the places I dropped flowers off had five or six servants. I went into the trade entrances of the apartment houses, and sometimes if I arrived at lunchtime the help invited me to join them.

I got an earful of what was going on in the household, much as in the BBC television series *Upstairs, Downstairs.* In most kitchens I visited, the butler and the cook had equal status. They sat at opposite ends of the table. The maids, many of whom had just arrived in the U.S. from Ireland or other European countries, scurried around to make sure that the butler and cook were happy. When the buzzer rang, the butler responded, unless it was one of the children. Then he sent a maid. The help had nicknames for the ones they served such as His Nibs, Her Nibs, Thumbsucker, and Facelift.

Food was forced on me, and in exchange I was expected to tell them about the other families to whom I had delivered flowers. I told the same story to everybody. "I once delivered flowers to a family on Long Island and they had this sad little boy who the servants suspected had been kidnapped by his wicked French nanny and brought to the United States, where he was sold to this family who couldn't care less about him, and he cried all the time."

Everyone believed me, particularly since by this time I told the story so well.

I discovered that funerals were the best place to get tips. I entered the funeral home or the house of the bereaved with a spray or a wreath. All the mourners were watching me. I took my time putting the spray at the head of the coffin and then moving it to the foot. The longer I fiddled with the flowers, the more nervous everyone became. Finally someone—a relative or friend—dug into his pocket for a tip just to get me out of there. I am aware I took advantage of people's grief, but if I had left it up to the funeral parlor employees, I would have never gotten a quarter.

Besides the good money they brought me, funerals fascinated me. I observed the person in the coffin, which was usually open, and I tried to figure out who he or she was and why they were dead. I also studied the behavior of the bereaved family and friends. The Italians and the Jews cried a lot. The Episcopalians were much quieter.

Delivering flowers to homes and funeral parlors was my introduction to death. I didn't know any of the people, but I still felt a sense of loss.

For a humorist, I think a lot about death. During both my depressions, I contemplated suicide. My main concern about my death was that I would not make the *New York Times* obituary page. I was sure it would be just my luck that Charles de Gaulle would die on the same day and all the space would be taken up with tributes to him.

The *New York Times* is the only institution which has the power to decide if you existed or not. You can spend eighty years on earth and if they don't say anything about it when you pass away, your life has been a waste.

In my depressed state, I wondered how the *Times* chose the five or six people who made the obituaries. Sometimes the page recognized a Bronx school teacher and other times they wrote up a Nobel Prize winner, or a former chairman of New York's United Jewish Appeal.

I never saw any people listed who had committed suicide. I wondered if they had a rule on it, like the Catholic Church.

I might have devoted so much time to the *Times* obituaries because of my days delivering floral wreaths and sprays in my youth or because I wanted some recognition. All I asked was for the *Times* story to say, "Hey, everybody, guess who was here and guess who has now gone?"

Depressions are cruel things and if a person is egotistical

enough and in a suicidal frame of mind, he methodically plans his own funeral.

In my head I held mine at Adas Israel, a large synagogue on Connecticut Avenue in Washington. (I also envisioned a memorial service in New York conducted by Tom Brokaw, John Chancellor, and Walter Cronkite.)

I saw my casket in the aisle draped in an American flag, guarded by six Marines. The synagogue was jammed and many people, even dignitaries, had to stand out on the lawn. Henry Mancini flew in from L.A. with his orchestra, and Isaac Stern came down from New York to play.

The rabbi led the congregation in prayer (I gave him a B)—then Ben Bradlee spoke, followed by Katharine Graham, Bill Styron, and Mike Wallace. In my mind, they all did very well.

It was a typical Washington funeral, with everyone checking their watches to find out when they would be out of there.

I used to cry when I imagined my funeral, with big tears streaming down my cheeks. It could have been the depression that made me do it or I could have been mourning for myself.

My first depression took place in 1963, shortly after I returned to the United States from Europe. It required a month of hospitalization and weeks to recover. It wasn't easy to admit that such a thing could happen to me—after all, I made people laugh. Funny men like me were supposed to be immune to the serious blues. But it wasn't so. Things were so bad at first I was even placed in a psychiatric ward. I was certain I would never laugh again.

But a funny thing can happen to you in a depression. If you don't hurt yourself, you can gain tremendous insights and empathy, find inner strengths and hidden talents. It's a mysterious process, but if you can hold on, you become a wiser and better person.

That's why, when the second depression hit me in 1987, I wasn't as frightened. It was just as vicious as the first, but this time I knew I could come out of it a stronger person, and I did. I was able to throw off all kinds of baggage from my childhood.

Bill Styron and I had depressions within months of each other. Once we recovered, we teased each other about whose had been the stronger. I claimed that mine had been a 9.9 on the Richter scale, and he said I had suffered nothing more than a rainy day at Disneyland.

What I didn't tell him was that I planned to have Isaac Stern play at my funeral.

I was still many years from such thoughts, however, as I took my flowers around. Once I took flowers to Elsa Schiaparelli, one of the great French designers. World War II had just begun, and she arrived from Europe to stay at the Hotel St. Regis. I rode the elevator to her floor and knocked on the door. When she opened it, the room was full of flowers, so she said, "Give me the card and take the roses home to your mother." She gave me a quarter.

I was quite excited to come home with two dozen roses. But Aunt Rose thought I had stolen them from the shop. She was convinced of it when she asked me the name of the woman who had given them to me, and I said, "Elsa Schiaparelli." She sent me to my room for making things up.

Many years later, at a dinner party in Paris, I related to Schap the tale of the red roses. She said, "That's the sweetest story anyone has ever told about me."

Each job not only provided me with spending money, but also gave me a chance to travel all over New York. At fourteen, I knew almost all the streets and I knew every inch of the subways.

Once I picked up three West Point Cadets on the subway. They were strangers to New York, and I offered to be their guide. They wore summer dress white uniforms and looked very sharp. Think of an Army cadet version of *On the Town.* I was proud to be in their company. People paid attention to West Point cadets, and for a few moments I was no longer the invisible man. We were getting along great, until they met three girls in front of the Hotel Astor on Broadway. They told me that they had seen enough of New York and said good-bye. That bothered me, because I still had the planetarium to show them.

Ever since reading *Catcher in the Rye,* I have identified with Holden Caulfield. I always believed that while he was working one side of the street, I was working the other.

New York was as great a movable feast as was Hemingway's Paris. For me it was the most exciting place in the universe. Since I didn't have a normal home life, I went into the city for all my nourishment. It was a different Manhattan from the one today.

Back in 1975, I met a friend named Walter Thayer on Broadway and 47th Street. He was an executive with the *New York Herald Tribune,* and we started chatting. There were bums sitting with their backs against the wall, drinking cheap wine while others were sleeping. Suddenly, one of them shouted, "There he goes," and all the bums drew their guns. They were undercover cops, and they started to chase one man running into the subway, and we heard a cop shout, "Stop, or I'll shoot." I couldn't believe we were in the middle of all this. It was like appearing in a bad gangster movie.

Years later, I wrote an article about New York being an

unsafe place to visit, and Walter, who was on a committee to boost the city as a tourist attraction, wrote me a stinging letter, taking me to task for overplaying the crime situation.

I wrote him back, "After the wild afternoon we shared together on Broadway, you are the only person in New York City who has no right to write me such a letter."

5

The First Time

Back in Hollis things weren't going too well for me. I had graduated from public school and was going to the Jamaica High School Annex. I was fourteen years old. My sisters had grown up, and since Alice and Edith were both working, my father took an apartment in Forest Hills, a posh neighborhood for affluent Jewish people.

The apartment he rented for seventy-five dollars a month even had a doorman in the lobby.

It wasn't easy to make the rent. As usual, Pop was earning very little money. Alice and Edith were barely earning any.

There was one other thing wrong with the place. We had an apartment, we had a doorman, but we had almost no furniture—the living room was completely bare. Furthermore, we had no money for furniture, and so Pop and the girls made do with a few beds, a kitchen table and chairs. The flat was a vast wasteland.

When my mother had been taken away, he'd placed all his

furniture, dishes, and linens in a warehouse. But he couldn't keep up the payments on the storage so the belongings had been sold.

Despite the lack of furnishings, we wanted to be together. At least I *thought* I wanted to be in my own home with my own family. All the foster homes were no more than halfway houses for the day when we would have our own place.

The reason I had begun to act up in the foster homes was that when the time came for us to be together, my own family wouldn't take me with them. They left me in the Devries home. Until that moment, I hadn't really minded living in a foster home—but as soon as the girls and Pop took their own place, I was very hurt. This was a major rejection. I started misbehaving, and Aunt Rose complained to the social worker that she didn't like me anymore, because I wasn't the boy she thought she knew. My grades fell, but I didn't care. I felt completely left out of everything.

"You were mad at us," Edith told me, "but we couldn't do everything at once."

Alice explained, "We thought that you were better off with Aunt Rose, at least until we got some furniture."

I told them, "I was terribly hurt and angry."

Edith said, "How could we know? You were always smiling."

When I told Doris about how disappointed I had been at the time, she said, "I told you not to expect anything from anybody."

For all that, my relationship with Aunt Rose was warm. According to the records, we got along very well and she even wanted to adopt me. But Pop turned down the idea.

Finally, when I reached fifteen, my father agreed to take me. I didn't know what to expect when I moved in. But I didn't find what I was looking for. My sisters were bossy, and I was not used to anyone telling me what to do. The accommodations were incredibly cramped. Pop and I slept in the breakfast room.

I hated school. I was fifteen and already having my first midlife crisis.

I began to look back on my foster homes with nostalgia, and I yearned to leave Forest Hills and enter the real world, if I could somehow find a way to get out of school.

For years I had lived in a house, and an apartment took some getting used to. Everyone was on top of everyone else and you could smell exactly what the entire floor was having for dinner—yet we were all strangers. Neighbors did not talk to one another—even when we took the same elevators. By anyone's standards, this was quite a nice apartment house, but there was no joy in the halls. I found the place very confining, emotionally as well as physically.

Our building was a few doors from Nat's Grocery. The reason I'm telling you this is that my father bought all his groceries from Nat, and it was there that he almost cornered the entire peanut butter market during World War II. Nat was a one-man operation, but he was a wily salesman. During the war, my father used to stop in every night.

One evening, not long before D day, Pop walked in and Nat said, "Mr. Buchwald, I'm not supposed to tell you this, but my supplier has just informed me that the war is coming to Forest Hills. There is going to be the worst peanut butter shortage this country has ever seen. I can't sell you more than four jars." My father told me he blew up and said, "How can you treat me like a nobody? I have a son in the Marines, I'm making blackout curtains for the government. I've been your customer for years."

Nat relented and sold him six jars.

Two or three times a week, Pop walked into Nat's and, without exchanging a word, the grocery man handed him six jars of peanut butter in a brown bag. When I came home from the war, the hall closet was jammed with peanut butter.

I said, "What are you doing with all this stuff?"

My father put his finger over his lips and said, "Shhhh. Nat says the country's running out, but he will always take care of me."

My social life was built around Forest Hills High School. We had these cliques and spent all our spare time together. My best friend was Bob Markay, whose father owned a handbag company. The Markays lived in a beautiful apartment and I thought of them as very rich. I was over there all the time. Mr. and Mrs. Markay were exceedingly nice to me and we stayed close to the very end of their lives. I trusted Bob so much that he was the only one of my friends I permitted to come up to the empty apartment. I knew he wouldn't make judgments.

The Forest Hills girls were something else again. Many were pretty and spoiled and wanted to go to the best places and seemed to be very much into material things.

The gang talked about the girls a lot. We discussed those who we were sure wouldn't do it, those who might if you got them excited enough, and those who, if you owned a car, would do it on the revolving stage of the Roxy Theatre.

A few pals (not me) had steady girlfriends, and they never discussed if their girls would or would not do it, or ever had.

The real truth is that almost all the girls in Forest Hills that we knew had not done it, because if they had they wouldn't be able to land a husband.

I had several dates with a pretty girl named Esther Berkowitz, who let me know right from the start that she wouldn't. But she hinted that perhaps after we got married and she got to like me, she might think about it. Her parents liked me very much and were sure that we would make a good match. I didn't know this for a fact—I sensed it. As soon as I suspected this, I called it quits. Nice as she was, Esther was not part of my future plans.

The two most important things to happen to me when I moved to Forest Hills was that I got a job in the mail room at Paramount Pictures in New York City, and I lost my virginity.

While attending high school, my dream was to work in New York City. When school ended at three o'clock, I went into Manhattan knocking on doors. One of my stops was the personnel office at the famed Paramount Pictures Building on Broadway at 43rd Street. It was famed because it housed the Paramount Theater, which featured every great band and singing star of the time—as well as first-run Paramount films.

The personnel office had a glass door on which was painted the name "John O'Connell." When I saw the name, an idea came to me.

I went in and declared to the lady at the desk, "Father Murphy sent me." I had uttered the magic words. The secretary immediately ushered me into Mr. O'Connell's office. He rose to greet me warmly. "How is Father Murphy?" he wanted to know.

"He's just fine and he sends his best. He thought that you might have a job for one of his students—part-time of course."

Mr. O'Connell, who loved Father Murphy as much as I did, assumed that we were talking about the same man. He said, "I don't see that as a problem. We could use someone from four to eight when everyone else goes home. It pays eight dollars a week and you are also entitled to two passes to the Paramount Theater."

I had the job of my dreams, thanks to a Jesuit priest who never was.

When I came home, my sisters couldn't believe it. One asked, "Why did you use a trick like that to get a job?"

"It wasn't a trick. Every Irishman in the world is honored to do a favor for Father Murphy."

For me, the job was a godsend, particularly since I was so disenchanted with high school. At five, all the mail room boys went home and I was in sole charge of picking up and delivering letters and packages and running errands for the people still left in the building. Most of the top executives worked late and over the course of time they got to know me. Leonard Goldenson, who later became head of ABC Television, sent me out for sandwiches from Lindy's. Neil Agnew, the vice president, was married to Arlene Francis, and had me pick up her dresses for her. I delivered scripts to famous directors and actors at their hotels.

I saw Dorothy Lamour at the Plaza once wearing a negligee. Cecil B. deMille received a script from my very hands at the Waldorf Astoria. I delivered airline tickets to Bing Crosby and a cheesecake from the Stage Delicatessen to Billy Wilder.

I felt like a big shot—happy and respected. Even the chairman of the board, Barney Balaban, trusted me.

At the end of World War II, I was walking down the halls on the ninth floor in my Marine Corps uniform when I ran into him in the hall. He asked me what division of the Marines I was in. I told him, "I'm an ordnance man in a fighter squadron." His face lit up and he said, "I'm glad I ran into you. I'm thinking of purchasing a private plane as soon as the war is over. Could you tell me what to buy?"

I told him that I didn't know what he should buy, but he

would be very unhappy flying around in a F4U fighter plane. It had only one seat.

The passes to the Paramount were as good as gold. Even the stuck-up girls from Forest Hills were impressed with them. On my hot date I whipped out the passes to the woman in the glass booth, and as she inspected it with suspicion I winked at the girl I was with. Occasionally I was able to sneak my date backstage, where performers such as Frank Sinatra, Tommy Dorsey, and Artie Shaw hung out. It was the equivalent of getting into the locker room of the Brooklyn Dodgers. What's more, I got my first great taste of show biz.

My Paramount life was so heady that school became even more uninteresting. The two subjects that I could never conquer were math and French. My solution to this was to cut classes. I attended English faithfully and wrote compositions that got me A's. I also wrote a radio column for the *Forest Hills Beacon.* And I was involved in high school politics, acting as campaign manager for a girl on whom I had an immense crush and who was running for president of the student body. We won the election, but I still wasn't happy. I had no focus, and there didn't seem to be any person to give me one. No one in Forest Hills was happier than I was to see World War II come along.

When the war started, they opened the Stage Door Canteen on 44th Street, just a half block from the Paramount Building. I volunteered, and because I worked for a movie company, I was accepted. I was a busboy and a dishwasher and did anything they asked of me—with other busboys such as Alfred Lunt, Bert Lahr, and Ethel Merman. I found rubbing shoulders with the famous and talented a very good experience, and one I still enjoy.

When I went off to war in 1942, Paramount treated me as one of her sons—sending me cigarettes, a newsletter, and a chin-up package containing a razor, toothpaste, and a photo of Dorothy Lamour. I was very touched by the attention and dreamed of going back to the mailroom when I returned to America in triumph.

My part-time job brought me home after dinner, and one evening I bought a potato knish from a vendor stationed in front of the post office in New York, where I deposited the last of Paramount's daily mail.

The knish was filling and very, very heavy. It sank directly from your mouth to your stomach with a thud. Only my strong stomach prevented it from continuing on to my feet. From then on that was my dinner.

My sisters' recollections of those days at Paramount are different from my own.

"You worked very hard," Edith said, "and when you came home you did your homework."

Alice said, "We never saw you. You were a stranger."

"Like the invisible man?" I suggested.

"Pop came in late, also. We always kept something on the stove in case you were hungry."

"As long as we're talking about Forest Hills," I said, "what did you girls do about inviting dates up to the apartment?"

"I almost died," Edith told me.

Alice said, "We made them wait downstairs. No one ever made it upstairs."

Edith continued, "The doorman used to call up when the boy arrived. He was a very mean person and he always said, 'Can I send him up?' "

"On several occasions, I told him he could drop dead," Alice said.

Then I raised something that I had been thinking about for some time. "You were very fussy about your dating—almost prudish. How do you explain that?"

"Aunt Stella was very strict with us. When we lived with her, she rarely let us go out on dates. She drilled it into our heads that we were nice girls, and most boys weren't nice boys," Edith said.

Alice agreed. "It all comes from the home. We never let a date do anything we would later be ashamed of."

I had asked the question because I wondered where my three sisters learned about romance, love, and companionship. They rarely talked about boys in front of me. If they liked one, they went out of their way to see that I didn't meet him, because I would always say something disgusting like, "She hasn't eaten all day," or, "Don't waste your time. Pop's trying to marry her off to someone rich."

In due course, all three of the girls got married and produced remarkably well-adjusted children, who will probably be reading for the first time about their mothers' childhoods as they really happened.

I am now ready to reveal how I lost my virginity. I believe that an autobiographer should only include information about his or her sex life if it contributes significantly to understanding what makes the author tick. I don't know whether it's normal or not, but sex has always been something that I take seriously. I would put it higher than tennis on my list of constructive things to do.

Which brings me to the "Summer of '41," when I was fifteen years old and was hired to run an elevator at the Hotel Nassau in Long Beach, Long Island. The Nassau was a large, aging building which had been a jewel in the early 1900s. It took up a block of the boardwalk and was the center of action in the area. The hotel was eight stories high—seven floors for the guests and the top one for the help. That's where I lived with two dozen other employees, and it was here that I received a unique education.

After a couple of weeks running an elevator, I was made assistant night clerk, which meant I checked people in between the hours of midnight and eight in the morning. The orders were quite specific from management, "If they have luggage, charge them the regular room fee. If they don't have any luggage, double the rate." People with luggage might argue about what they were being charged, but people without luggage NEVER questioned how much we were charging.

I recall a couple checking in without bags. They registered as Mr. and Mrs. Lee. As I was getting their key, the man said to the woman, "Cigarette?" and she replied, "I don't smoke."

I was also introduced to another kind of life, because many of the hip college kids from West End Avenue in New York City hung out on the beach in front of the Nassau. I was impressed with the way they carried themselves, the way they dressed, and the way they smoked cigarettes. I took it all in, and decided that they were the greatest bunch of people I had ever met. Years later when I thought back about them, I said to myself, "What a bunch of assholes."

Let's move on to the top floor of the Nassau. A chambermaid lived in the next room. Her name was Anna. It doesn't matter what her real name was. Anna was in her thirties. Though her face was slightly worn from making so many beds, she had something important going for her—she had very full breasts. She wasn't a beauty, but I don't know too many guys in my circle who lost it to someone resembling Rita Hayworth.

I was walking down the hall one afternoon and Anna came

out in her bathrobe and invited me into her room for a glass of wine.

We talked about the hotel, and the manager, who demanded a lot more work out of the chambermaids than they could deliver, and exchanged information as to the best suntan lotion to use.

As I sat on the bed, I felt perspiration on my forehead. I dared not look at Anna, so I stared at her legs. They were beautiful. She held my hand and read my palm. "You have a very warm heart." Suddenly, we were clutching each other on the bed. As we kissed, it dawned on me that this was the moment that I had waited for all my life. Other times, women had led me down the garden path, and snatched me from the gate at the last moment, but this time I was certain that I would score.

It happened a lot faster than I wanted it to—actually, before I was able to take off my pants. So Anna, dear Anna, gave me a second chance, which shows what a good person she was. I have no idea where Anna is at this moment. Sometimes I imagine her making a hotel bed somewhere and leaving a chocolate truffle on someone's pillow.

I hope she thinks of that never-to-be-forgotten afternoon when the waves pounded on the surf eight stories below us as we were quickly bathed in perspiration on that squeaking bed in her non–air-conditioned room. I have often wondered whether she knew that I had come to her pure as the driven snow. I did not experience great pleasure—I was too frightened to feel anything—but it was one of the most meaningful moments of my life. And Anna will always have a large page in my memory book.

My first time was no big deal, but the repercussions were

tremendous. When I came home from the hotel and bragged to my sisters that I had lost my innocence, Edith said, "You dirty boy."

Alice said, "Aren't you ashamed of yourself?"

"Why should I be ashamed if I did something beautiful with someone who enjoyed it?"

Edith said, "You're only a baby."

I responded, "I may be a baby, but I made love to a thirty-one-year-old woman."

Alice said, "Suppose she gets pregnant."

"She can't," I told her. "I used a Trojan."

Edith screamed. "Big shot. He can't even pass algebra, but he knows how to use a Trojan."

Alice said, "You're despicable."

"I'm not. I just got lucky. Everyone always does it with an older woman the first time."

I concluded that my sisters' problem was that they had no idea of what to do with a brother. They felt that they should watch over me, but they were dealing with a loose cannon. The idea of me, at the age of fifteen, having an affair with a woman was too much for them to grasp. They knew that telling my father would be useless, because he'd only say, "You dasn't do it."

I received a better reception from Arnie Alperstein and Bob Markay in Forest Hills, who wanted to carry me down Queens Boulevard on their shoulders. I was the first one in the gang who had gone all the way with a woman. It was more important than if I had discovered the Salk vaccine. I wish I could say on the basis of this experience that I was in demand as a stud and that women have fallen all over me ever since. It wasn't to be. Anna gave me a good start. She felt, and rightly so, that after that afternoon I was on my own.

I don't think that it's relevant to give too many further

reports on my love life. Of course, there have been good times and bad times. As a person whose life has been dominated by matriarchs, I have always been afraid of hurting women. I never wanted them to think less of me. On one particular occasion, I got credit for a beautiful evening in which I did not participate.

I was on a USO tour of the Philippines in the sixties with Al Capp, the cartoonist, and George Plimpton, the writer. Capp, who was one of the great Lotharios of our time, picked up a nurse in the officers' club at Clark Field and disappeared with her for the evening.

Twenty years later, I was attending the Democratic National Convention in Atlanta and a lady came up to me and said, "Remember me?" I didn't.

She continued, "You and I had that fantastic evening at Clark Field."

"That wasn't me," I protested. "That was Al Capp."

"No, it wasn't," she insisted. "It was you. I don't forget things like that."

I was so shaken that I called Plimpton and yelled, "Did I go to bed with a nurse in Clark Field or did Capp go to bed with her?"

"It was Capp. I remember it because I lost seventy dollars to you at gin rummy."

I never saw the woman again, but I assume that she'll go to her grave convinced that I was the person who brought her whatever pleasure she had in the Philippines.

I know that in today's sexual climate, you shouldn't brag about losing your virginity. You shouldn't even admit that you ever lost it. But in the early forties it was a remarkable achievement that has stayed with me as one of my least painful experiences.

6

Flossie and the Marines

The infamous attack at Pearl Harbor on December 7, 1941, came as a shock to Forest Hills. A group of us, including Bob Markay, George Hankoff, Arnie Alperstein, and Dick Zimmerman were in the bowling alley on Austin Street when the news flashed over the radio. First there was disbelief, followed by serious discussion of what would happen next. We were all sixteen years old—and we were certain of everything.

Arnie said, "We'll beat the hell out of them in two weeks."

Bob Markay agreed. "Our fleet will sink the bastards and then they can kiss our ass."

Everyone at the bowling alley was certain of the brevity and outcome of the war, and fearful that it would be over before we could serve our country.

Let me state that most of the ethnic references about the Japanese and the Emperor used at the time would not be considered politically correct today. But in those days after

Pearl Harbor, it was permissible to call the Japanese anything you wanted to.

Our group was not too well informed about Japan, except that their soldiers were very short, had gold teeth, and raped Chinese women. We knew that they owed their allegiance to the Emperor and didn't give a damn about their own lives, preferring at the slightest excuse to slit their stomachs open if they thought they had disgraced their country in any way. Before the war they had made very cheap toys that always fell apart and, therefore, we concluded that if their war equipment was of the same quality they were doomed to defeat.

Our knowledge of the Germans was much better. Those of us raised in Jewish homes had been briefed by the adults about what a butcher Adolf Hitler was. Throughout our lives, we were told to pray that he and his supporters should die a thousand deaths while being eaten by wild dogs.

One of the things that has puzzled me all my life is that every Jewish family in America knew what Hitler was doing to their relatives—but President Roosevelt didn't appear to know and neither did anyone else in the government. Was it a question of not believing what they heard or was Hitler one of those pre-war embarrassments?

Forest Hills was angry. While my friends were discussing Pearl Harbor as the country's problem, I took it personally. It dawned on me that the Japanese attack could be my ticket out of high school. The country needed manpower, and the call to arms was resounding over the air waves every half hour. I was prepared to lie for my country and say I was eighteen so I could avenge the treachery of Pearl Harbor. No one ever mentioned it, but thousands of men welcomed World War II as a way to escape their humdrum lives rather than a chance to fight for God and country.

The next morning, on December 8, bright and early, I went down to the Naval recruiting station in lower Manhattan. The line wound three times around the block. It was a sight to behold. There were men in double-breasted suits and young recruits in overalls. Every color of skin was represented. There was an excitement in the air. The enemy had struck the first blow—now the men in line were prepared to reply in kind.

I stood in front of two boys from Brooklyn.

One said, "They say thousands were killed at Pearl."

The other one responded, "Roosevelt will never tell us, because he blew it."

"I hope I get on a submarine," I told them. "You sink a lot more ships on a submarine than you do on the surface."

The first Brooklyn boy said, "My brother's in the Navy and he says he gets more fuzz than he can handle. Women are crazy about sailors and they're not going to refuse you when you're prepared to die for your country."

Now this interested me very much. "How do you get your pants off in the Navy?" I asked. "They all have funny buttons on them."

"You learn that the first week. My brother is stationed in San Diego, and he has to beat the dames off with a broom."

Then I said, "Maybe with a war on, they'll keep the women away from us."

He shook his head. "No chance. Things will be even better than before Pearl Harbor for servicemen. I know a girl in Brooklyn who told me that if I come back in uniform, she'll go all the way as soon as I walk in the door."

"Be careful," his buddy warned, "those are the kind that will make you marry them."

Unfortunately, the line moved at a snail's pace. An Army

recruiting sergeant moved up and down the line shouting, "No waiting to get into the Army—no waiting to get into the Army." The third time, I bit, and followed him to the Army recruiting station, which was down the block.

I filled out the papers, lied about my age, and was sent into a classroom to take a test designed to find out if I could read and write or had any emotional problems. The men surrounding me were not too bright and they kept asking me for the answers to the questions, which I was happy to supply.

I helped three recruits pass the tests, with flying colors. I am certain that they were the ones who captured Omaha Beach on D day, and were given battlefield promotions to the rank of colonel on the spot. After the test, I moved on into another wing of the recruiting station for a physical exam.

It was the first time that I had appeared naked in front of so many other men, and I was embarrassed. The Army was not too thorough about the physical, although one of the doctors called me on the carpet for biting my fingernails. He said that he didn't think he could take me unless I promised not to bite them. I agreed, but, frankly, I couldn't understand how you could be shot at with live bullets *without* biting your nails.

I passed everything and was informed that a letter would be sent to my parents requesting them to sign the forms permitting their son to join the service.

I wasn't quite certain how to handle the problem, but the next morning I stole the key to the apartment mailbox from my sister's purse. I intended to open the box before she got home and forge my father's name to the papers.

Sadly, my sister was sick that day and stayed home from work. She couldn't find her key for the mail, so she asked the superintendent to open the box. There she found the letter from the War Department (in those days you named things for what they were) and promptly went on a crying jag. When my sister Alice came home, she went on one also. My father didn't cry, but raged. He was so mad that when I walked in the door, he shouted, "You came by accident and you'll go by accident."

I have remembered that line all my life. It confirmed something that I had often suspected during my childhood. I really wasn't wanted.

I'm sure that my father said it in anger, but if there hadn't been some truth to it, he would not have said it at all.

It was a frosty gathering in the living room that December 9. Everyone started to yell at me at once. If patriotism is the last refuge of the scoundrel, then I was the biggest scoundrel in Forest Hills.

"Someone has to fight Hitler," I declared.

"Not children," Alice retorted.

"I am a man, and my country has been attacked by the Japanese. Do you expect me to stand by and do nothing?"

My father tore up the permission papers, and my last words to him that evening were, "I'll do it again."

With the war on, it was more difficult than ever for me to concentrate on high school. I cut classes all the time. I attended early matinees of war films and was completely inspired by the U.S. Marine movies starring John Wayne and Victor McLaglen. I wanted to be a leatherneck more than anything in the world and come back in Marine blues to Queens and show everyone what a real hero looked like.

That brings us to the "Summer of '42," which had a tremendous effect on my life. There was a resort hotel in New Hampshire called the Mount Washington Hotel, located (not surprisingly) at the base of Mt. Washington, on 10,000 acres of land known as Bretton Woods. In 1944, it would become famous when the economic geniuses of the world met there to decide what everybody's money was worth.

I was hired as a bellboy, thanks to my experience at the Nassau Hotel the previous summer. There were no questions asked about my race, creed, or religion, which was surprising. Not long after I arrived at the hotel, I discovered that the Mount Washington did not take Jewish guests. I can't be too sure how they felt about Jewish employees, although as the summer wore on I suspected that I was under heavy suspicion of being "one of them."

The reality of a restricted hotel was brought home very brutally to me one day, when a man arrived by taxi and I was sent out to carry in his bags. The manager on duty gave him a registration form, which he signed with a Jewish name. The manager blanched and said, "I'm sorry, Mr. Kaplan, I made a mistake. There are no rooms."

I knew that there were, and I sensed the problem was the man's name. He realized he was in the "wrong" place and asked, "Could you call me a taxi?"

The manager replied, "I'm sorry, but all our phones are tied up."

"I'll get you a taxi," I said. I went to the phone at the bell captain's desk and called for one. Then I stood with the man on the porch in the heat for an hour, waiting for it to arrive. He told me that he was a salesman passing through, and that it was the first time something like this had happened to him. I was too ashamed to say I was Jewish, too. The brave thing would have been for me to have left with him. I didn't. I expected to get fired, but the owners of the hotel liked me, and it was hard for the manager to do anything except be nasty to me for the rest of the summer.

The hotel guests were very fancy people, including American oil tycoons such as the Sun Oil Pew Family, and the president of Tiffany's, and assorted blue bloods who preferred the mountains to Southampton.

I was very uncomfortable about my situation, but I didn't have the guts to call it quits. I liked wearing a uniform and I enjoyed the people I worked with very much. I particularly enjoyed the company of a waitress named Flossie Starling. She was a student at the University of North Carolina at Greensboro, and she drove me mad with her Southern accent. There was no place to go at night except the woods or the hotel golf course. The boys and girls slept in separate dormitories and the rules were, you couldn't enter one if you didn't live there.

Flossie and I got into heavy petting on our first date. It took place on the eighteenth hole of the golf course, only several inches from the cup. Flossie would not give me any sexual favors, but it didn't matter because I fell in love, and since I knew that we would someday marry I could wait for her most precious gift. At Mount Washington, I claimed to be a freshman at Columbia University, which was the only reason Flossie would have anything to do with me. The other reason was that there were twenty-five boys and seventy-five girls working at the hotel, and the one to three ratio played in my favor.

We climbed Mt. Washington by moonlight, splashed under waterfalls, and picked wildflowers in the meadows. By day I wore a dashing uniform, and Flossie was dressed in an immaculate waitress outfit that could not camouflage her glorious body.

Some guests were easy to get along with and some were impossible. We could deal with the latter if they tipped well—usually they didn't. The help seemed like family. We had students from Gallaudet, the school for the deaf in Washington, D.C., working as dishwashers. One day the Gallaudet students taught sign language to several of the boys. We then spoke to each other using our hands, which made the girls furious. So they learned it, too, and in no time the deaf students became part of the gang.

I was checking the rich high society in, enjoying the role of a Columbia freshman and in love with an older woman who made me gulp every time she said in her Southern accent, "Would you please pass the meat loaf?"

The summer went by, and before we knew it, it was time to go back to where we'd come from. Flossie and I parted in an embrace, vowing that no matter what happened we would always love each other. I don't recall if there were tears or not, but the message we whispered to each other was clear. This was the beginning—not the end.

So I went back to Forest Hills, no longer a Columbia freshman, but a high school senior disgusted with every phase of my life and constantly thinking of Flossie. In October, a few weeks before my seventeenth birthday, I decided to take action. I planned to run away from home and join the U.S. Marine Corps. I was not just going to join the Marines—I was going to make it into a movie scene. I chose to head South to North Carolina and say good-bye to Flossie, just as I imagined it would happen if I directed it for the silver screen. Flossie (played in the film by Jennifer Jones) would beg me not to go. But I would tell her somebody had to stop the yellow peril and their craven ally, Benito Mussolini, as well as the U-boats that sank ships loaded with innocent people and vital war cargo.

The script called for Flossie to say I had to choose between her and the Marine Corps, and I would reply, "My country right or wrong."

At the end of the fantasy, I would be standing on the train

with my head out the window. The train's whistle would sound as we pulled out of the station. Suddenly, Flossie would be running along the platform. She'd yell to me, "I love you, my darling Arthur. Come back alive." Then she would disappear in the swirling steam from the engine. Cut. That's the way I planned my entrance into the Corps.

I started hitchhiking South, leaving word on the kitchen table that I was going to enlist in the Army. When I passed near Fort Dix, I mailed a postcard to my family which said, "Well, I got in. I love you." My intention was for them to look for me only in the Army, which would keep them away from the Marines.

As I was on the road, my sisters launched a search for me. My trick worked. The Army was where they were trying to find me. Alice told me that she called Fort Dix and they turned her over to a sergeant. She was panicky—he was calm. He made her spell my name, then came back and asked, "Is he colored?"

She burst into tears. Alice quickly discovered that the military couldn't care less about underage boys joining up. They took them gladly and kept them, unless someone made a fuss about it.

I arrived in Durham with enough money to rent a room in a boardinghouse. It was six dollars a week, which included breakfast. The boarding house also came with a voluptuous owner's daughter who had never bundled with a Yankee before, and although her mother didn't know it, she included herself in the price of the room. In true Southern style, the breakfasts were banquets. It was the only serious meal I had all day. There were meats, grits, eggs, waffles, jams, and Southern biscuits. These breakfasts were in a class with any meals I have eaten in Paris.

Mother

Pop

Uncle Oscar, Mother holding Edith, Alice, and Pop.

Julius Gartner (far right) and Pop (third from right) at the raincoat factory during World War I.

At the Seventh-Day Adventist Home. Doris is second from left; I'm at the far right. I don't remember who the two other kids are.

The four of us with Pop. Left to right: Edith, Doris, Pop, me, and Alice.

Many years later, in Kings Park, Jamaica. I'm thirteen, Edith is next to me; Doris and Alice are in front. Doris and I were living at the Devries house now.

With my cousin Eddie Lampner (right) at the HOA's Camp Wakitan.

The bellhop of Bretton Woods, New Hampshire, 1942.

The Marines made a man out of me. On Eniwetok, 1942.

Flossie Starling, 1943.

With my third foster mother, Aunt Rose Devries, while on leave in 1945.

At USC in 1946. The clerk said, "Fill this out," and I was in college.

With David Wolper and two friends at USC.

Jane Russell engrossed in the USC humor magazine *Wampus,* which I edited.

With friends at the bar of the Hôtel des États-Unis, Paris.

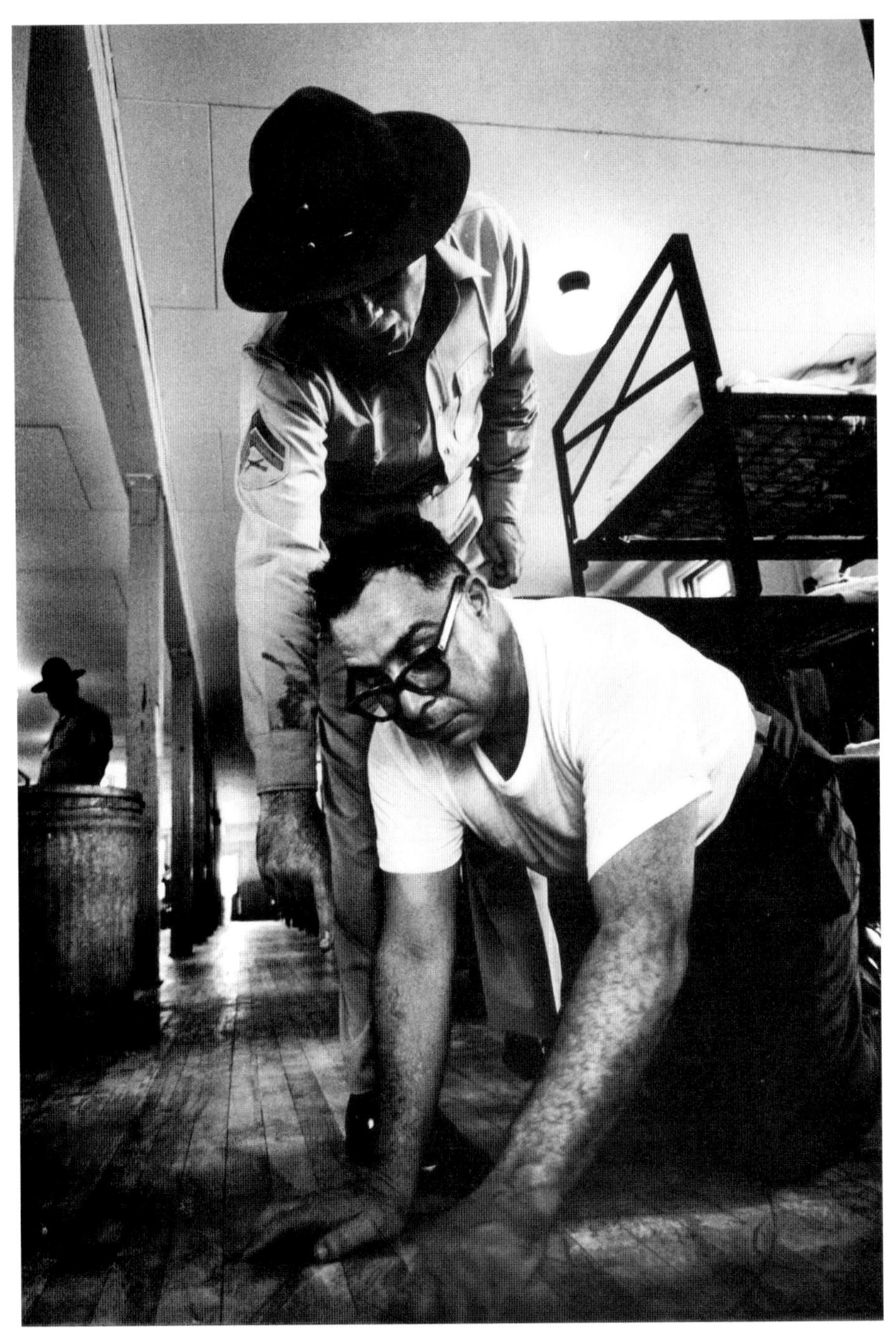

Twenty-five years after boot camp, my drill instructor, Corporal Pete Bonardi, and I returned to Parris Island for *Life* magazine. Here, he explains to me what a clean floor does for a Marine (Bob Gomel, *Life* magazine. Copyright © 1965 Time Warner).

To earn some money, I took a job in a meat-packing plant. I was stationed in the refrigerator. They put a very, very heavy overcoat on me and assigned me to a butcher's block. My job was to scrape meat off bones, which was sold for stew.

The fridge was freezing and my fingers immediately went numb, so while I scraped the bones I noticed pools of blood on the block. It didn't take long for me to realize that it was my blood.

By the fourth day, all my fingers were bandaged. At the end of the week, I concluded scraping meat off bones was not what it was cracked up to be. I had enough money to keep moving and said good-bye to Durham.

I never wavered from my goal, which was Greensboro, North Carolina, where Flossie was attending the university, which at that time was an all-girls' school. It was a Friday afternoon when I arrived at Flossie's dormitory. My surprise was complete. She couldn't believe that I would show up without notifying her.

I was wearing a leather jacket and a dirty shirt and all my fingers were bandaged. I hadn't intended to look that bad, but I assumed Flossie would feel sorry for me. She demanded to know what I was doing there. I told her that I hitchhiked all the way from New York to say good-bye to her before enlisting in the Marines.

"Did it ever occur to you I might have other plans?" she asked.

It hadn't.

"A boy from VMI is coming down this weekend for the Fall Hop, and I am going out with him."

"Don't those nights on the eighteenth hole of the golf course mean anything to you?" I asked.

"That was summer," she replied, in an exasperated voice. Then she said, "Do you want to go to the dance with my roommate?"

"I don't have a tuxedo."

"Pete d'Angelo, the orchestra leader from Mount Washington, left his with me."

Later on, while I was overseas, it dawned on me that something was going on between Pete and Flossie. Otherwise how did the tuxedo get in Flossie's room?

I was so desperate to be near her that I agreed to go to the dance. I had one more problem besides the fact that the tux didn't fit very well. I had no black shoes. I took five dollars and went to a secondhand store in Greensboro and bought a pair. That left me just about enough money to pay my bill at the YMCA.

The night of the dance, Flossie breezed into the ballroom as gorgeous as I had ever seen her, with the VMI cadet in dress uniform at her side. I, on the other hand, was fighting to keep Pete's tux on. It was too big for me and I kept getting lost in it. There were a few close moments when I thought I would lose my pants. Flossie's roomie liked me just as much as I liked her, which communicated itself in stony silence. I never heard a word she said, because my eyes were always on Flossie. No one has ever accused me of being Fred Astaire, so I couldn't even put the VMI guy to shame with my jitterbugging.

The dance ended and we went to a roadhouse for hamburgers and milkshakes. There were about three other couples with us. The VMI twit had a convertible, and my date and I piled into the back seat. I sat on a pint of liquor. Feeling its shape with my hand, I made up my mind that Flossie's lips would never touch the bottle and I placed it where I could steal it when I left the car.

At the roadhouse, everyone was polite but cold. Along with everything else I had to worry about—I had no money to pay for my share of the food. I had spent my last five dollars for the black shoes. When the check came, all the men threw in their share. I sat—a block of cement with a red face—looking into my glass. They all stared and then someone quietly threw in my share. Flossie was furious and my date was humiliated. And so we rode back to the YMCA in silence. It was then I committed my final despicable act of the evening. I put the pint of whiskey under my shirt and, without saying good night, walked to the YMCA doors.

The next morning, which was Saturday, I woke and realized that I had no choice but to enlist in the Marines, and the sooner the better. I knew the recruiting office was at the post office, so I arrived at nine.

A tough Marine Corps sergeant was sitting behind his desk.

"I want to join the Marine Corps," I said.

"How old are you?"

"Seventeen."

"You have to get your parent's permission."

"No problem," I assured him. "Dad's in town now buying feed for the farm. Just give it to me and I'll see that it gets signed."

"It has to be notarized."

"No problem," I told him. "I'll see to that."

He gave me the papers and then growled, "We close at noon on Saturdays."

I was out in the street on Skid Row trying to work this one out in my head when a tiny, grizzled man stopped me. "Would you give me a dime so I can get a drink?" he whined.

"I'll do better than that," I said. "I'll give you a pint of whiskey."

"What do I have to do?" he asked suspiciously.

"I'm trying to get into the Marines and my dad won't let me. If you become my father for just thirty minutes, I'll give you the whiskey."

The old man's bloodshot eyes crinkled up and he said, "Why, that's patriotic."

Someone steered me to a notary and I said, "Can I talk to you privately?" He took me into the other room.

"My dad's been drunk for a month and I'm trying to get into the Marine Corps. Would you have any objection if I steadied his hand while he signed the papers?"

"I'll do anything for someone going into the Marines," he said.

We went back and I held the drunk's shaking hand so that the signature read, "Joseph Buchwald."

Racing against the clock, I ran back to the YMCA and gave the old man his pint of whiskey. Then I ran down to the post office and at five of twelve delivered the papers to the sergeant.

"How long do you need to get things in order?"

"I am ready to go this minute."

He shrugged, swore me in, and gave me a bus ticket to Raleigh, food coupons for two days, and a voucher for a seedy hotel.

I called Flossie. "Flossie, I'm at the bus terminal and I'm leaving for Parris Island to fight for my country."

Flossie said, "You behaved terribly last night. I've never been so ashamed in my life. You also stole Fred's bottle of liquor. I don't ever want to speak to you again."

I could tell that she was mad and that she had no intention of coming down to the bus station to see me off. In spite of it, I hung my head out the window as the bus pulled away from Greensboro, hoping that at the last moment Flossie would come running alongside and crying, "I'll wait for you." And that is the true story of how one of America's fine young men wound up in the U.S. Marine Corps.

There is a happy ending to this story.

Years later, I received a call from the University of North Carolina at Greensboro, which was coed by then, asking me to speak at their commencement. They were unaware of my previous connection with the school.

I said that I would love to be their speaker. Instead of giving the boilerplate pabulum, my entire talk was about my 1942 adventure at the school. I spoke of Flossie with warm affection and of my drunken "father" with great nostalgia. I described everything just as I have here. The audience was transfixed. It was unlike any school speech they had heard before. I was assured afterward by several graduating students that the story of Flossie would inspire them in their future life. The faculty thanked me for making the commencement one to remember. No runaway had ever had the opportunity to return to the scene of one of his greatest humiliations and be received with such acclaim.

There is a second happy ending to this story. I heard from Flossie the other day and she's not mad at me anymore. She asked for my forgiveness.

I replied to her letter saying, "Nothing new on the war front. The Japanese lost Midway and Guadalcanal and are now begging for mercy. The war should be over soon. You're forgiven."

7

The Marine Recruit

People are constantly amazed when I tell them that I was a Marine. For some reason, I don't look like one—and I certainly don't act like one. But I was, and—according to God, or the tradition of the Corps—I will always be a Marine.

The skepticism about my military background keeps haunting me. Not long ago, I attended a Gridiron dinner in Washington, D.C. This is a very fancy white-tie affair given by the Washington press establishment. One of the highlights of the evening is when the U.S. Marine band plays the anthems of the four military services.

When their anthem is played, the people who served in that particular armed force rise from their seats and stand at attention. When the band struck up the Marine Corps hymn, I stood up.

I heard one of the guests sitting across from me say to his dinner guest, "What is Buchwald standing up for?"

The other man replied, "He was a Marine."

The first man said, "Jesus Christ!"

Despite what others think, I earned my stripes as a Marine. At the same time, the Corps gets full credit for straightening me out. At seventeen I was young, I was unhappy, and most of all, I was undisciplined. The Marine Corps was the right service in the right place at the right time.

My military hitch was a three-year experience, which I think about a lot. It was also a very painful one, which is exactly how the Marines intend it to be.

First, there was the bus ride from Raleigh to Yemassee, South Carolina, the last stop before you hit Parris Island. The trip should have been uneventful, but it wasn't. There were eight or nine recruits from the Raleigh area on the bus.

I was seated halfway down the aisle. An elderly black lady with a tattered suitcase at her feet stood leaning over me. I got up to give her my seat, which she refused. The bus driver, who was watching in his mirror, stopped the bus. He came back to where I was standing and said, "You sit back in your seat, you stupid son of a bitch, or I'll throw you off the bus." Then he did something really weird. He apologized to the lady for my rudeness. I wish I could tell you that I stared the driver down, but I didn't. The old lady moved farther back so that she wouldn't be standing next to me. For her I was trouble. What made matters worse was that my fellow recruits tried to avoid me. Later they accused me of letting the Marine Corps down.

When most people think about civil rights, they picture Martin Luther King, Jr., speaking at the Lincoln Memorial. I will always remember that little old lady on the bus and how I had failed her. I didn't know what else to do. If I had been thrown off the bus, I would have missed my scheduled arrival at Parris Island.

I'm not sure what the Marines would have said if I told

them, "Sir, the reason I'm two days late is I had to hitchhike because I was thrown off the bus for giving a black lady my seat because I didn't know it was against the law. I'll never do it again."

It was a long ride after that, and I spent it looking out the window as we sped past the towns of the South. I saw for the first time the "white" and "colored" signs outside the restrooms and on the drinking fountains. I noticed black people bent in the fields and tethered thin dogs barking at our bus. It all made me think of *Tobacco Road.* I felt as if I were back in the second balcony watching Will Geer peeing on the stage.

Later on I ran into a different kind of black person. (I'm slightly in trouble here because in those days the good guys called black people Negroes.) The Marines had allowed blacks to enlist, and they were full-fledged members of the Corps, with one exception: they were segregated in their own units. On Eniwetok in the Pacific, we had an anti-aircraft unit composed of black leathernecks. We had nothing to do with them because they were bivouacked off by themselves. One day I was down on the beach gathering shells, and I got to talking to a couple of them. I asked what they did and they told me. Then I asked if it bothered them that they were separated from the rest of us. One fellow replied, without sarcasm, "Sheet, no—we're Marines."

We arrived at Parris Island at three o'clock in the morning. As soon as I got off the bus with the one small bag I was permitted to bring, people in pressed khaki uniforms and pointed hats covering their pointed heads started to yell at me. At that hour of the morning, the non-commissioned officers looked even more forbidding than they were in the daytime—but not by much. The NCOs alternated between cussing and personal epithets. We were told to line up, and then we were ordered to get on the bus and go home because we would never make effing Marines. They said that we were all bedwetters, and that we were dying to get back home and suck our mothers' tits.

Then they marched us off to our barracks, where there were two-tiered beds with mattresses, but no sheets. It was four o'clock in the morning by this time. The man in khaki yelled, "Go to sleep, you mothers" (I have left out most of the cussin', since it was used so frequently that your eyes would eventually glaze over).

Parris Island was turning out U.S. Marines as fast as they could—and then after a little more training at advance bases, the recruits were being shipped off to places like New Guinea, Guadalcanal, Bougainville, Tulagi, and other unheard-of paradises in the South Pacific.

That was the little picture, which didn't concern me too much. I was only involved with the big picture—my survival at P.I.

In every Marine's life there is one man he remembers as long as he lives—and that is his drill instructor. The DI has a singular role and that is to take raw recruits and turn them into fighting machines. He does this through threats, psychological terror, physical exercises, and hazing, which is only used when no one is looking. The whole process is built around fear.

When you first enter the Corps, their only goal is to reduce you to a stuttering, blubbering bowl of bread pudding. For starters, they shear all the hair off your head, so that no one can tell you from any of the other recruits in your platoon. They issue you clothes and equipment that has to be kept spotless, and finally they hand you a rifle, which you must revere and guard at all times.

The brainwashing never stops and you are subjected to it

morning, noon, and night. No matter what you do right, you are told that you are doing it wrong. The DIs rip up your bed after you worked on it for an hour. Your shoes are never shined enough, your foot locker is judged to be a mess, and your replies to questions are never satisfactory. You are constantly told what a hopeless, miserable, mother-fornicator you really are. Only the person who bore you could love you. The purpose of all this is to break you down, and then rebuild you into the person the Marine Corps wants—one who will never question an order, who will always worry about his buddy, and who, someday, will walk as tall as John Wayne.

My drill instructor was Corporal Peter Martin Bonardi of Elmhurst, Long Island. Every Marine who goes through boot camp claims in later life that his DI was the toughest, meanest son of a bitch in the whole United States Marine Corp. It was no contest—mine was. Don't listen to other Marines. Trust me.

What made life even more difficult for me than for the other recruits was that I was a Yankee in a Southern platoon. Therefore, I was the perfect goat. Bonardi called me "Brooklyn," and was constantly running up to me and screaming in my face. His term of respect for me was "Private Asshole."

I was punished in the day and I was punished at night. The most serious crime a Marine recruit can commit is to call his rifle his gun. The rifle is worshiped in the Corps and, despite the Corps' wealth of tanks, missiles, and airplanes, the rifle is still considered a Marine's most important weapon. If you drop it, you have to sleep with it that night. If you drop several while stacking them—the rifles sleep in your bed, and you sleep on the floor.

Once I made the mistake of calling my rifle a gun. Bonardi sent me up to the outdoor landing on the second floor of the barracks. He yelled, "Drop your pants!" Then he yelled, "Now raise your rifle in one hand and hold your pecker in the other and shout, 'This is my rifle—this is my gun.' "

I stood in this position for two hours, yelling out across the parade ground, "This is my rifle—this is my gun."

I had no problem gathering a crowd. DIs with their platoons made special detours to parade by. When they got to me, the NCOs halted their troops and ordered them to look at what a dumb sheethead really looked like.

Another time, I marched in formation past a recruit in another platoon, and he had a pail on his head which he was banging with a scrubbing brush. He was shouting, "I am a shitbird." I made a mistake and laughed.

As soon as we got back to the barracks, Bonardi ordered me to get a pail and brush. Then he told me to put the pail on my head and start shouting, "Hoohoo, hoohoo, I am a shitbird, too."

Bonardi never ran out of tortures. He made me clean the barracks head with a toothbrush. Then he forced me to march around the barracks with rocks in my pack, because I was brushing my teeth when he called everyone out for muster.

It doesn't take long before your DI becomes the most important person in your life. I was more afraid of him than I was of all the things the Marines required us to do. For example, when I saw the Parris Island obstacle course for the first time, I froze.

Bonardi told us that the course was easy. We had the choice of doing it or going to sick bay and having his boot removed from our ass. It was his way of motivating us. I completed the obstacle course—not once, but twice. Bonardi never even said thank you.

Late one afternoon, when I was doing fifty pushups on the

parade ground for having failed to polish my shoes so "I could see my face in them," a thought occurred to me.

I would go to Bonardi and confess to him that I had enlisted in the Marines by fraud. I would tell him that my real father had not signed my enlistment papers, but I had gotten an old drunk off the sidewalks of Greensboro, North Carolina, to pretend he was my parent. A handwriting expert would certify I was telling the truth.

Therefore, I would tell Bonardi, I was not a legal enlistee and they had no choice but to discharge me.

I never followed through on my plan, because I had a terrible idea what the consequences would be if Bonardi refused to investigate my story. I also didn't want to leave because I believed there were far worse things waiting for me at home than pushups.

Meanwhile, back in Queens, the search for me was on in earnest. My whereabouts were discovered accidentally, when my foster mother, Aunt Rose, boarded a bus in Jamaica and ran into my elementary school English teacher, Mrs. Egorkin. While in boot camp I was writing to her, because I had to write to somebody, and I felt she was safe.

Mrs. Egorkin did not know that I had run away and was surprised at the news. She gave Aunt Rose my address, on the condition that she not tell my father where I was unless she had my permission.

Aunt Rose wrote, describing all the agony my sisters and father were going through. She urged me to give her the right to tell them where I was. I agreed, but said that any attempt to get me out of the service would only mean that I would run away again, and this time they'd never find me.

The Marine Corps was not my father's first choice for me. I think he would have preferred the school traffic monitors in

Forest Hills. But he realized that I meant what I said, and so he decided to let me stay.

My father, while quite certain that I was in tremendous danger, was still proud of my enlistment. Edith told me that a few months after he acquiesced, he had to complete an order for blackout curtains on Governor's Island off Manhattan. He had forgotten his pass, so when the guard stopped him, he produced my picture in uniform and said, "My son is in the Marines. Do you think I'm going to blow up your fort?" They let him in.

I was finishing up my tour at P.I. All of us in the platoon had hardened physically. There is nothing like a twenty-mile hike with a full pack and one canteen of water to convince you that you can not only lick the Japs, but the U.S. Army and Navy, too.

On graduation day, Platoon 911 marched together for the last time on the parade grounds of Parris Island. In eight weeks, the D.I.s had accomplished their mission impossible. We may not have been seasoned Marines, but we looked like seasoned Marines. For the first time, Bonardi smiled at us before he said good-bye. We knew he was pleased, because he had won money on our performance from the drill instructor training the platoon in the next barracks. I vowed that I would never see him again. It turned out that I did.

In 1965, I received a telephone call from George Hunt, the editor of *Life* magazine. He asked me if I was interested in going back to visit Parris Island, and write a piece about it. I said that I'd like that, but it would be better if I could find my DI, Pete Bonardi, and we returned together. Hunt said that he liked it. (He was a Marine, too.) I called Marine Corps headquarters and asked them for the last address they had on Pete Bonardi. They gave the one in Elmhurst. I looked him up in a Queens telephone book, and damned if he wasn't still at the address of twenty years ago.

I dialed, and a male voice answered, "Bonardi."

I said, "I don't know if you'll remember me or not, but this is Private Buchwald from Platoon 911."

"Yeah, I remember you. I was sure you'd get killed."

"I'm sorry, sir. I'm still alive. I'm calling about returning to Parris Island to do a story for *Life* magazine, and they thought it would be a good idea if you went with me."

"I'm working at the World's Fair," he said gruffly.

"I'll get them to spring you for a week. It will do you good to see the place again."

Bonardi said that he would go if I could get him off without losing his job.

He hadn't changed. Physically, he looked the same. I was still in awe of him. When I was in therapy, I tried to examine all the different influences the Marines had on me. In dreams, I always had a Marine arranging transportation for me, getting me out of jams, and saving me from life-threatening adventures. I concluded that the Marine Corps and Bonardi figured very largely in the accounting. I also began to realize that the Marine Corps was the first father figure I had ever known. From early morning to late at night they took care of all my needs. It was a love-hate relationship, as many father-son ones are. I mentioned this to a master sergeant who was escorting us, and he said, "Fifty percent of all recruits coming through here feel the same way."

It was twenty-five years since I had been to P.I. Not much had changed. The only difference was that this time I was less frightened. I was also amused at the way Bonardi observed the scene. He was furious about how soft the training had become, and amazed that you could no longer spray saliva in a recruit's face when you yelled at him.

He was filled with nostalgia as we walked around. "Hey, do you remember when I caught you with your hands in your pockets? I made you fill them full of sand and sew them up, and you were carrying fifteen extra pounds around for a week."

"Those were the good old days," I responded.

"You were really a shitbird," he told me with warmth.

"You always told me that."

"It wasn't my fault. When I said 'eyes right,' I wanted to hear them click. And when I said 'eyes left,' I wanted to hear them click. I never heard your eyes click."

"I wanted them to click, but they never would."

They put me in a platoon of recruits who had no idea what I was doing there and never asked. I was issued the boot uniform and I did many of the things the platoon was involved with. Bob Gomel, a photographer from *Life* was at my side, and Bonardi went back to his old role. Some of the trauma returned. It was hard to believe that I was able to do all the various physical tasks on the schedule. The obstacle course now seemed like Mount Everest. I made a pass at it and fell in the mud. Bonardi yelled at me. "Twenty-five years ago, I would have hung your testicles from that tree."

"How could I have made the course in the old days?" I asked him.

"Because I was always by your side, darling, saying things like, 'If you don't do it, you yellow pissant from Brooklyn, I'll have you clean the floor with your tongue.'" What I always loved about Bonardi was that he used reason when he talked to you.

For a week I did as much as I could, but the fear wasn't

there, because I knew I was leaving. The one thing I noticed was that they now had black drill instructors. They were the meanest of the mean, the toughest of the tough. This was long before Lou Gossett played a DI. But I was impressed and so were all the boots. I heard later that the platoon I had hooked up with at P.I. all went to Vietnam—the first Marines to arrive there. They were very, very young—but then, I thought, so were we.

Bonardi and I finished our week's tour, and both agreed that the present DIs were a bunch of bleeding hearts and were turning recruits into debutantes.

We shook hands at the Savannah airport and said good-bye. We never saw each other again.

There is a final chapter to my relationship with my drill instructor. In 1991, I received a call from a man who said, "Your pal Bonardi is dying from cancer. He is at the hospital in Southampton, Long Island."

I called the hospital and spoke to him. He told me that he was very sick and he didn't think he was going to make the obstacle course. After I hung up, I remembered the photos taken by *Life,* which were in the files. I took out one of the two of us, nose to nose. I wrote on it, "To Pete Bonardi, who made a man out of me. I'll never forget you." And signed it.

His wife wrote to me and said that Pete put it up in his hospital room so that everyone could read it. The clincher was that just before he died, Bonardi requested that the photo be buried with him.

It was.

8

Ordnance Man

I have never known whether life was one big crap shoot or a stud poker game. My experience as a Marine convinced me that there was someone deciding my destiny. I have no problem crediting the God of Abraham with choosing my fate—although on some days I have been certain that some clerk in Washington has played a major role in my life when God took the day off.

What happened was that either a person or a machine in personnel at Marine Corps Headquarters split our boot camp platoon in two. One half would go into the infantry and the other would be ordered to Marine Corps Aviation.

When the news was read out to us in our final formation at Parris Island, those who were assigned to the air wing were chagrined. We had joined the corps with one purpose—to kill Japs. The Marine bureaucrats were depriving us of this privilege. There was disbelief that our role in the war would be a minor one. We would never hit the beaches as we had seen in our favorite films. It wasn't as if we were going to fly planes. We would be ground crews, with not one chance of glory. It would be impossible for any of us to win the Medal of Honor.

The lucky men in our platoon were ordered to Camp LeJeune for wallowing in the mud and on the beaches. They were destined to plow through malaria-infested jungles and charge the enemy on heavily defended pieces of coral, planting Old Glory wherever it had to be planted. Their names would be chiseled on stone monuments and they would have their division flags hanging from Marine mess halls. We envied them—for they were blessed. The fact that most of them were killed or wounded, and our half of the platoon escaped unscathed, was not considered at the time.

I recall that after the assignments were read to us, I went to see Bonardi and said, "Sir, when I enlisted, the recruiting sergeant promised that I could be a paratrooper."

"Okay," Bonardi said, without looking up, "you're a paratrooper. Now get out of here."

I don't remember if I said good-bye to Bonardi the day I left his custody. I am certain that he didn't choke up when I boarded the train. For a moment, I did have a fantasy of him running alongside the train as we pulled out, yelling, "I love you, shitbird—I love you."

It was a long ride to Cherry Point, North Carolina. The train left at four in the morning, about the same time we had first arrived as green recruits with no idea what we were getting into. Now we were leaving, salty boot graduates at least ten feet tall. It was dark and spooky at the Yemassee station, and on the other track I saw a trainload of pitiful recruits arriving and lining up as I had eight weeks before. The Marines on our train started chanting, "You'll be sorry. You'll be sorry."

We heard one of the new recruits cry out, "I already am."

The only thing missing in my departure scene was Flossie. I imagined her on the platform searching the crowd frantically so that she could tell me how proud she was that I had finished boot camp and was now going to destroy the Rising Sun. I yearned to hear her tell me how sorry she was for turning her back on me at the University of North Carolina, and I wanted to hear her say that she would pray for me every night and kiss my photo on the nightstand before she went to sleep.

They say that people enlist in the military for the most patriotic of reasons. Don't believe it.

One night in the barracks, a bunch of us were discussing why we joined.

One boy said, "I did it because I didn't have anything better to do."

A second said, "I joined because my brother said I wouldn't."

I said, "I did it for a woman."

I had their attention. I was almost tempted to recite "The Face on the Bar Room Floor."

"She was a Southern girl with an accent like thick molasses, and she had breasts the color of peaches. She said that her only role in life was to make me happy. She also said that she would never love another as she had loved me. Then she left me for a VMI cadet who owned a convertible and was drunk all the time."

"What was her name?" someone asked.

"Flossie, Flossie Starling. I have a friend, Arnie Alperstein, who warned me about Flossie. He didn't know her, but what he said fit most of the women I have known. He told me, 'Whenever you see a beautiful girl, remember this. She is a pain in the ass to somebody.' "

The train arrived at New Bern, the town just twenty miles

from Cherry Point—a giant base which had become the main Marine Corps air facility on the East Coast. After Parris Island, Cherry Point looked as beautiful as Tahiti. We were free men. We could go to the PX, the slop shoot (for beer), and the movies without asking permission. We didn't have to say "sir" to non-commissioned officers. For a few days, until I got bored, I couldn't believe that I had so many choices.

Best of all, I began smoking cigars. My father always smoked cigars and I liked the idea of sticking one into my mouth whenever I felt good. I averaged eight cigars a day in my prime and maintained the habit until I was fifty-nine years old.

During those years people complained about the smoke, but even at dinner tables, I thought nothing of lighting one up at the end of a meal. Friends pretended that it didn't bother them, when it did.

In the Marines I smoked very cheap ones—White Owls or Robert Burns. But as time went on, I upgraded my smoking habits until I was puffing on Davidoffs from Cuba, and Dunhills from the Dominican Republic.

One of the greatest honors of my life was to be elected "Cigar Man of the Year," a distinguished award presented by the Cigar Manufacturers' Association. The payoff for attending the dinner was that I was given a year's supply of Havana cigars. (This was before the United States put an embargo on Cuban tobacco.) I might mention that President Kennedy loved good Havana cigars—the day before he announced the trade embargo that led to the Cuban missile crisis, he had his press secretary Pierre Salinger stock up on enough Havanas to keep both of them happy for years.

I tell you this because cigars became a very important part of my life—they were my pacifier, my security blanket, even my Valium. Whenever I was feeling good, I put one between my lips, and whenever I was feeling bad, I lit one up.

If someone asks you a question, you can stall for as much as twenty seconds to give a reply by inhaling and then slowly withdrawing the cigar from your mouth, and letting the smoke come out.

When I suffered my first depression in Washington in 1963, I was certain that I would never write again, nor would I ever be able to make people laugh.

Listless and sad, I found myself sitting at my desk a week after being discharged from the hospital, tapping nothing particular on the typewriter. Then I pulled open the center drawer of my desk and saw a cigar there. I hadn't smoked the entire time I was depressed.

I stared at it for a moment, and then unwrapped the cellophane and stuck it in my mouth. Finally, after chewing on it for ten minutes, I lit it, and suddenly my fingers moved across the keys as if I were playing a Chopin sonata. I wrote a column about Jackie Kennedy getting pregnant, which meant that all the women who wanted to be in fashion had to get pregnant as well.

Everything had come back. The connection between the cigar and writing was so strong I couldn't do one without the other.

That afternoon I walked into Dr. Morse's office puffing on a Dunhill with a big grin on my face.

At Cherry Point, I was assigned to ordnance school, which meant that I had to learn all about guns, bombs, and torpedoes. I hated guns, bombs, and torpedoes—not because I had anything against their purpose, but because I had no idea how they worked and I had never had any mechanical aptitude. I kept telling the instructor to put me in something else before I endangered the pilots. But he was ordered to turn out ordnance men no matter what the cost.

To give you an example that I knew what I was talking about—a year later, I was in the Central Pacific, loading a 500-pound bomb on a Corsair fighter plane. I pushed the wrong thingamajig and released the bomb from its rack. It plummeted to the ground, just missing my foot. Everyone along the flight line either headed for bomb shelters or hit the deck.

I realized I was in trouble, so I dropped to the deck and screamed, "My foot, my foot, I think I broke my foot."

Someone called for an ambulance and before they could organize a lynch party I was transported to the hospital. The doctor took X rays and said, "There is nothing wrong with your foot." I said, "Doc, if you release me now, you're going to have to issue a death certificate. Please keep me here overnight."

He did, and I escaped the squadron's wrath. I mention this incident as only one of dozens that prove even the Marine Corps can make mistakes when it decides who should be handling our country's weapons.

From Cherry Point, I was sent to Memphis for more schooling. The Memphis Naval Air Station was under water the entire time I was there. The reason was that a Memphis political kingmaker named Boss Crump had sold the Navy acres and acres of swamp and had made a bundle on the deal.

Only two memories of Memphis still exist. One was that I failed to salute a WAVE officer. The guys in my group muttered some sexist remarks about her, making sure she would hear them. I didn't say anything, but since I was grinning ear to ear, she lit into me and chewed me out in front of all my friends.

This all happened in 1942, and my buddies said that I was chicken shit and I should have told her to buzz off. I said that I could be court-martialed for not saluting an officer, and they claimed that with an all-male jury I would have beaten the charges. The worst thing I could have gotten was a bad-conduct discharge.

The second incident which stays with me was more ominous. I picked up a girl in a Memphis bar and she took me back to her hotel room. She had once been pretty and she was lonely. I stayed with her several times. One afternoon, I pulled open a bureau drawer and found four syringes inside. I wasn't up on the drug scene, but I sensed something was wrong. She behaved funny and used to send me out on errands for things that she really didn't need. When I came back, she hardly knew I was there. I told someone about the syringes and he said, "Jesus Christ, she's using dope. Stay away—far, far away."

I still think about her, because I have always wondered how she got on drugs and where she bought it. I assume it was heroin. She was so damned fragile. What bothers me was that hardly anyone in those days took dope—I certainly had never heard of it. So she was hooked at a time when very few people were into that scene. I wished I could have helped her.

I received an advanced diploma in ordnance from Memphis, which gave me credentials to load ammunition onto anything that could fly.

My next assignment was the El Toro Marine Base in California. The railroad was the accepted form of troop transportation at that time. They used to hook our troop cars onto the regular trains. On this particular trip west, as we pulled out of

Memphis, the most beautiful girl I had ever seen walked by with a perspiring first lieutenant. That evening she returned on the way to the dining car with a major, and by the time we left St. Louis she was being escorted by a colonel.

My friend Ackerman, who was cleaning his shoes, said, "I'll bet you by the time we get to Albuquerque, she makes general."

El Toro was the West Coast equivalent of Cherry Point, but it was located in Orange County amongst the sweetest-smelling orange groves in America. Laguna Beach was a few miles away, and had been taken over by officers. The enlisted men prowled the streets of Balboa and Newport. Whenever we got bored, we hitchhiked into Los Angeles. If you're going to fight a good and just world war, every young man should be stationed in L.A.—at least once.

I always believe that someone was trying to make it up to me after Memphis by sending me to Los Angeles.

This was 1943, and men and women clung to each other desperately—to say either hello or good-bye. It wasn't a question of who was nice and who wasn't. The men were far from home and the women were falling in love left and right. In many ways people felt much more unconstrained during wartime than at any other period.

Some Marines were more successful with dates than others. The greatest success story I have ever known was a barracks mate named Danny Dooley. He never failed to return from leave without claiming he had "scored."

I maintained that he was lying and had to strike out once in a while. But he just smiled and said, "No way." Then he said, "Come out with me and I'll let you see for yourself." I agreed to go. We went to the Biltmore Bar in Los Angeles on a Saturday night. It was packed with women, and a few men in uniform.

Dooley and I were happily talking to two attractive secretaries when the bartender announced that the bar closed at midnight.

One of the girls suggested that we return to their place. I thought it was a great idea, but Dooley said, "Listen, I think that I should tell you something. I can't make it with a girl."

We all laughed. Dooley's eyes watered and he said, "I'm not kidding. I have never been able to make love to a woman."

Dooley's girl said, "Don't worry. We'll just sit and talk."

When we reached the apartment, I sat on one couch with my date, and Dooley sat across from us with his girl. I watched in amazement as she said to him, "Dooley, put your hand under my blouse."

He pushed her hand away. "It's no use," he cried. "I'll only get you all excited and then you'll be frustrated."

She took Dooley's hand and put it on her breast. "Now," she said, "doesn't that feel good?"

Dooley just shook his head as she moved the same hand to the other breast.

Meanwhile, back on my couch, I placed my arm around my date. She threw it off. "Not so fast, Charlie," she said. "What do you take me for?"

"A nice girl, a beautiful girl, the girl of my dreams. What's wrong with holding you in my arms?"

"You're treating me like someone you picked up in a bar."

While this dialogue was taking place, Dooley's girl was unbuttoning his uniform, rubbing his chest, and urging him to trust her.

My girl turned to me and said, "I think you better go."

"Don't you like me?" I asked her.

"I like you very much and that's why I don't want to do something I'll be sorry for." She held the door open and I was out on the street. The last glimpse I had of Dooley was his head in his girl's lap, yelling, "You can try anything you want, but it won't do any good."

I sat on the curb outside the apartment house waiting for Dooley to come down, trying to figure out what I had done wrong. An hour later, he descended and said quietly, "She thinks she saved my life."

It has been many, many years since that night. But every time I go to Los Angeles I remember it. When evening falls, I gaze up on all the lights of Los Angeles and think, "I wonder how many women out there believe that they made a man out of Dooley?"

I was assigned to VMF 113, a fighter squadron that flew the F4U Corsair—one of the most beautiful planes of World War II. The wings were designed like a gull's and the pilots said that it was the best aircraft ever made.

VMF 113 was made up of seasoned veterans of Guadalcanal, both pilots and enlisted personnel who had fought the early battles in the Solomon Islands, as well as greenhorns like myself. Our CO was an ace named Major "Doc" Everton who had shot down ten Japanese fighters. Many of the veterans had returned to the States with severe cases of malaria, which they could never shake off. Our assignment was to get the squadron shaped up so that we could return to the Pacific.

My duties involved loading and cleaning the .50 caliber machine guns. This was not the most difficult job in the U.S. Marine Corps, except for someone like myself, who, when it came to cleaning anything, had a very short attention span. But sincc I never complained, I was promoted to corporal, which was the equivalent—so the Marines maintained—of making major in the Army.

One of the heaviest burdens I have carried over the years

involves the day I saw a man die when I was at El Toro. I was out on the runway stretching a target sleeve on the ground, when a plane piloted by a first lieutenant landed, bounced several times, and then flipped over completely.

I ran toward it with two other ordnance men. The pilot was hanging upside down from the cockpit by his safety belt and a fire had started. Instead of rushing in to save him, which would have meant getting badly burned, I stood on the side and did nothing. Finally, the fire truck arrived and a man in an asbestos suit pulled him out. I later heard that the pilot died. To this day, I've asked myself if I committed a cowardly act by standing by—or whether I should have been a hero and dashed in without weighing the cost.

At a squadron reunion in 1991, I discussed the incident for the first time with Sully, my master sergeant. He told me, "You don't remember, but I was out there with you laying target ropes. I was also faced with the same choice. I didn't go in, and to this day it has haunted me." I felt somewhat better knowing that someone else had been troubled by the same decision.

The men all knew that we would soon be departing for overseas, so we took as much leave as we could. I usually headed for Beverly Hills and upper Sunset Boulevard. First, I was hoping to meet movie stars, and secondly, the people in the film business did not see too many servicemen, and when they did they were quite nice to us.

I would go to a ritzy restaurant like the Players, owned by the director Preston Sturges, and order a beer. Then when some patriotic civilian said to me, "What are you drinking?" I would reply, "Scotch."

I had not been outside of the States yet, but that didn't bother anyone, including me. I discovered that the more I clammed up about the battles I had fought, the more battles they thought I had been in.

One evening I was drinking late with four Marines at the Beverly Hills Hotel bar when a famous actor joined us. The bar was closing and he asked where we were staying. We said that we didn't have a place and he invited us back to the Garden of Allah, a famous apartment complex which housed many movie stars. We accepted.

The actor assigned two Marines to the second bedroom and said that the other two could sleep on the couches. We were all drunk and went to sleep immediately. Some time later, I felt a hand, and then a head, by my crotch. I brought up my knee and heard a groan, and the person slipped off the couch to the floor. I went back to sleep.

The next morning when we got up, our host's face was very swollen. It turned out he had made a move on all of us and in each case he had been rebuffed with a knee. Nothing was said. We got dressed, drank some coffee, and left. The actor, who played very masculine parts, continued his career, but after that night for me he would never be as convincing as he had been in the past.

Most young men have had attempted homosexual experiences. The first time I was approached was when I was thirteen years old and I was hitchhiking to visit my friend, Billy Mahler, at Lawrenceville, the prep school in New Jersey. The man who picked me up said that he was a traveling salesman. He started to tell me stories about women he had seduced, and they were quite erotic and I became aroused. Then he put his hand on my crotch. I took it off and he put it on again. Luckily, in those days, there were traffic lights on U.S. 1. We came to one and I jumped out the door like a shot. I never told anyone about it, because I was afraid that I would be blamed for the incident because I had an erection.

I have been approached at other times, too, but have always managed to escape. The worst experience was when I was on a troop ship in the Central Pacific. The air raid alarm sounded, and I ducked into a door. A big fat Marine Corps master sergeant was standing there. He lunged at me and tried to kiss me. "Christ," I said. We struggled in silence. Then I remembered something. It was his testicles. I took my fist and hit him there as hard as I possibly could. The sergeant let go of me to hold his family jewels, and I ran for safety to another doorway on the ship.

What hurt me the most at the time was not that I had been sexually assaulted by a man—but by a Marine.

My most memorable love affair in the service took place with a widow from Canada. I haven't used her last name, because I recently heard that she is president of her bridge club in Ontario, and I don't want any of her members to know that she cavorted recklessly with a fighting leatherneck during the Second World War.

I met Gwen in a church basement in Santa Monica. She was standing by the punch bowl and I approached her and said, "I wonder if I could have a large glass, because I'm going overseas tomorrow to sacrifice my life for my country, which will be a terrible waste of my youth."

That was my favorite opening line when I attended a USO, and it got me attention.

Gwen was very pretty. She had light brown hair, blue eyes, and a lovely trim figure, and so we danced and we talked. Then she told me something that was very sobering. She said that her husband had been an American Royal Canadian Air Force pilot who was killed in a crash. She had a year-old son named Al.

She also told me that this was the first time she had gone out since her husband was killed, and I was the first man she had seriously talked to since then. It was heady stuff to absorb in an L.A. USO.

I saw her the next day and the next. We had picnics on the beach and we drove by movie stars' homes. We took her son in his stroller for walks, and we sneaked into the pool at the Beverly Hills Hotel. I'm not sure if I was in love or not, but the idea of being involved with a widow seven years older than myself was as romantic as anything I could imagine for myself at that time in my life.

I don't think that Gwen considered me a potential husband, but she told me that I had gotten her out of her depression and for that she would always be grateful.

When I went overseas, we corresponded. One day in Hawaii, I bought a coconut, which I mailed to her. It said, "Merry Christmas" on it.

It doesn't sound like a big deal, but it was. I lost touch with her until one Christmas Day in the sixties, when I was living in Washington. The phone rang—it was Gwen, and she wanted to review the entire relationship in Santa Monica, which she maintained was the brightest moment of her life.

Then Gwen said, "Do you remember that coconut you sent me from Hawaii?" I said I did.

"Well, I've got it on the mantel. I put it there every Christmas."

I was glad to get the news, but I wished to Christ that she'd get off the phone before my wife picked it up.

9

To War and Back

It wasn't easy to say good-bye to California in early 1943. I bade farewell to as many friends and strangers as I possibly could. I shook hands with bartenders and put my fingers to my lips, swearing them to secrecy concerning my imminent departure. I told Gwen and my other dates not to wait, but to marry someone else and, once in a while, whenever they saw a plane flying overhead, to think of me. When I didn't have anyone else to tell, I would say to the bartender while nursing a beer, "There was this girl named Flossie—Flossie Starling—and I joined the Marines because of her, and she doesn't even care that I'm sailing for some Jap-infested island jungle."

If the bartender showed sympathy, I would continue, "When I was leaving for Parris Island, she ran alongside the bus and cried, 'Arthur, I will wait for you.' She lied, like most Southern women do. She never wrote. Here's a picture of her. It was taken on the eighteenth hole of the golf course at Mount Washington in the summer of 1942. She's probably hooked up with some 4F who makes raincoats for the military." If they bought my story, I usually got a beer on the house.

I told the whole damn world that I was heading out to the Pacific. And I made them all promise not to tell anyone.

When I stopped at the USO for doughnuts and coffee, I would say to the person serving them, "I once knew a widow who served me coffee and doughnuts. I wonder if I'll ever see her again." The lady would usually squeeze my arm and say, "I know. I know."

One evening just before sailing, I was in a movie house in Beverly Hills with a date. The theater played a newsreel showing Marines landing on an atoll in the Pacific under heavy fire. At the end of the newsreel, the lights came on and some people spotted me in a Marine uniform. Damned if everyone in the theater didn't get up and give me a standing ovation. I tried to duck, but my girl held my hand as if to say there was nothing wrong with being a hero.

I finally stood up, waved my hand, and left the theater with my jaw sticking out, just the way I had imagined old Wayne would do it.

After the ovation, I was sure that I'd get lucky that night, but it didn't turn out that way. My date said, "You're too good for me." I have never told anyone about this particular theater incident until now. It was a part of war that I liked to keep to myself.

Finally, the day came to ship out. The squadron was packed, the planes were loaded onto an aircraft carrier, the USS *Bunker Hill*—a brand-new ship that provided plenty of deck room for sleeping, exercise, and playing touch football. It set sail for Hawaii, and those of us who had never been overseas before were very excited.

It was an uneventful trip, and the only noteworthy aspect of it was my assignment to brig duty. It taught me a lot about myself. There was one prisoner in the brig charged with stealing from a crew mate. On my watch the carrier had hit a squall and was bouncing up and down and rolling around, which made the inmate violently seasick. Our orders were not to talk to prisoners and not to do anything to make their lives comfortable. The brig rat was upchucking and begging me for some sort of help.

"I can't help you," I told him.

"Why not?" he cried.

"Because you're a loser." I looked through the bars and he was a pitiful sight. Later on, I decided anyone looked pitiful behind bars.

"I haven't done anything wrong," he protested.

"Bullshit," I replied. "You stole from your shipmates."

"I made a mistake."

Besides everything else, he was a liar. What has always worried me about this exchange was that I enjoyed it. I had the power. He was like the poodle I frightened with a leash. My prisoner was not an innocent, so I didn't have to feel sorry for him. "Shut the hell up," I warned him, "or I'll take the mattress out of your cell."

I did my watch. It was frightening, because I learned from this experience how easy it was to be inhumane to someone. I am not by nature a cruel person—in fact, I hate cruelty. But like most people, I can be influenced to behave cruelly in bad situations.

The Marines were tougher than other soldiers on Marine and Navy prisoners. I think it came from their training. Once I took a Navy prisoner up to Portsmouth Naval Prison after the war. I delivered him and then had lunch in the mess hall. The guards told me that if they didn't make their prisoners miserable, they would be thrown in with them.

Anyone sentenced to the brig was to be punished to the point that he would never want to go there again.

We disembarked at Oahu and were driven in buses to a Marine Air Base in Ewa.

There we trained some more. We had casualties far from the fighting. We lost three enlisted men when one of our Corsair fighters missed the runway and crashed into a head. All the victims were doing was sitting in the crapper. The question that went through my mind was how headquarters explained the accident to the next of kin. They probably made up some story about the men losing their lives while engaged in training for a dangerous mission against the enemy. I hope that their loved ones never found out what really happened.

We trained very conscientiously, because the squadron was determined to achieve glory by getting more Japanese Zeroes than anyone in the war. Our pilots were talented and morale was high. Also, everyone loved the Corsair. It reappeared on television years later, when they made a series based on Pappy Byington and his Black Sheep Squadron. Pappy was a misfit and so were his pilots—but they turned in the best record of downing Japanese planes of any Marine squadron. They became part of Marine folklore during the war and had a second life when the TV series was a great success.

Ewa wasn't one of the tourist havens of Hawaii. It wouldn't have been a town at all if it hadn't been for the Marine base. The reason we even went into town was because we could get our laundry done at very inexpensive prices by an old Japanese lady. The arrangement was successful, until word got around that she charged so little because she was a spy for Tokyo. We had no proof of it, but it was a good story. After the rumor, we were told not to have our laundry done by anyone who was suspected of worshiping the Japanese emperor.

Because Hawaii was sinking under the weight of the armed forces, we had no overnight liberty. We were permitted to go into Oahu at nine in the morning and we had to be back on base by six at night. As soon as they arrived, many GIs would get into line at the dozens of whorehouses in the red light district. The lines stretched for blocks, and reminded me of the ones at the Paramount Theater when Frank Sinatra was playing there.

When the servicemen got inside the front door, they paid a fee and then were attended to by an employee of the house in no more than five minutes, after which they exited via the rear door. Then they went shopping for presents for their mothers—and the girl next door. Nobody saw any contradiction in patronizing a whorehouse and then shopping for a loved one back home.

In war, one thing had nothing to do with the other. I'm not trying to cop a plea when I say that I didn't participate in this form of sexual gratification. For one thing, I hate standing in line for anything. For another, I get terribly nervous and can't perform if I know someone is standing behind me holding ten dollars waiting to make love to the same girl.

So I spent my mornings searching for gifts. When we had finished our shopping, the group would eat in a great Chinese restaurant or steak house. After which we would go to a bar, drink five or six beers, and then return to base. Some officers may have had "respectable" girls, but the enlisted men were not so privileged.

I am a big fan of Jimmy Jones' book *From Here to Eternity.* His Oahu was similar to the one I knew during the war, and I saw the movie several times. I guess the main difference between Jones' characters and us was that they were permitted to roam Oahu at will and we were kept behind the fences, except when we went in town. Also none of us looked like Burt Lancaster, so we never had a chance to make love to an officer's wife in the surf.

One day we were eating lunch in town when one of the men in the squadron, Armand Constantine from New Orleans, made a sage observation. He said, "One of the most amazing aspects of the attack on Pearl Harbor was that the Japanese bombers spared all the whorehouses in Oahu. They must have known their location, and the high command probably decided to keep them intact so that they would still be there when the Japs conquered the island."

We didn't stay in Ewa very long. One day, we were ordered to join up with a task force leaving for the Central Pacific. Our ship was the *President Wilson* of the President Lines, which had been converted from a cruise liner into a hot, smelly, groaning troop ship. It was very crowded, and half of us slept on deck so we could get some air. We also reasoned it was a better place to get off the ship if it was torpedoed than down below.

The *President Wilson* wound up with a unique crew. As we were loading the ship at a Pearl Harbor dock, a landing craft with about fifty men came toward the ship. The men were guarded by ten Marines. The Marines made their prisoners board the boat and MPs escorted them below. I found out at chow what this was all about. It seemed that the fifty sailors were so called "brig rats" who were constantly deserting their outfits so that they wouldn't be sent into combat. Pearl Harbor had had enough of them, so they had ordered the men put on our ship at the moment we sailed. The brass hoped that the men would finally make a contribution to the war.

It was a good idea for the Navy, but a lousy one for us. The fifty were incorrigible. After dinner they turned the fore and aft mess halls into gambling casinos. They set up crap tables and card games in every corner. The gambling was heavy because the attitude of the Marines aboard was that since they were going into combat, money had lost all meaning.

Had the brig rats just devoted themselves to gambling, the Marines might have put up with their behavior. But several days out, our rifles and pistols started to disappear. Stealing a Marine's rifle is worse than stealing his wife, and there were some very bitter exchanges between the rats and the Marines. They took place in the mess hall, when the leathernecks held the heads of the brig rats over steaming kettles of inedible food, and said things like, "If we don't get our rifles back in five minutes, we'll drown you in this sewage."

The message was loud and very clear, especially when the Marines made several brig rats commit fellatio on their bayonets. In a matter of hours, the weapons showed up and nobody drowned in the kettles.

When we were far enough from Hawaii so no one could hear us, our commanders briefed us on where we were going. Our destination was the Marshall Islands—tiny dots of coral necklaces, occupied by the Japanese. The news was worrisome from one point of view: our biggest losses in the Central Pacific up until then had been at an atoll called Tarawa. At that landing, someone had forgotten to check the tides, and the men coming ashore had to wade through 1,000 yards of water under deadly Japanese firepower. The Marines had been cut to ribbons. Thousands of leathernecks were killed or wounded.

Kwajalein was very similar in looks and the big question was: would we face the same kind of resistance? We were assured that the Naval Command was doing everything it could to prevent another Tarawa and had sent one of the largest armadas in the Pacific to shell the island. In fact, the lagoon seemed to be blowing up for three days and it was hard to believe anyone would still be alive. Some Japanese soldiers had survived the shelling, but the fighting was short and Kwajalein did not turn into a mess, thanks to the lessons of Tarawa.

I am not a military expert, but I like to read about war, especially World War II. I even have a theory about it. We seem anxious to revere wartime battles based on their heavy casualties. When generals and admirals screwed up, as they did at Tarawa, the invasion became a glorious victory in which many more brave men died than was necessary. Few think of it as a stupid bungle that should never have happened. Tarawa takes up chapters in history books. Kwajalein, on the other hand, has more or less been forgotten as a battle, and rates less than a paragraph in any telling of World War II.

The enlisted men of our squadron did not go ashore. We were held in reserve in case things went bad.

When the Marines landed at Kwajalein, which was the Japanese headquarters for the Marshalls, they found maps and intelligence indicating that Eniwetok, another coral atoll in the Marshalls, was weakly defended and could be taken with the reserve troops that had not landed.

So we sailed to Eniwetok, entered the harbor of the lagoon, bombed the hell out of the defenders, and on February 19, 1944, landed on its shores. The 22nd Marines secured the northern section of the atoll and we stood on the deck as the battleship and cruiser guns pounded the island of Engebi.

"Jesus Christ," said Carroll. "They're knocking down every tree on the island. We won't have any shade."

Pianowski said, "I don't care if they kill everybody, as long as they leave us some Jap souvenirs to take home."

Shulman said, "They're dug in deep, and they'll all come out as soon as the shooting stops."

I said, "The sailors on the battleships can sit back and keep throwing in all the shells they want, but we still have to go ashore and find out who is there."

Sully, who had been on Guadalcanal, asked me, "Are you scared?"

"Not me," I said. "I'm a Marine."

He said, "You're full of crap."

He was right. I really wanted to go home.

We gazed over this desolate rock with little joy. This was to be our home for the next twelve months. Engebi was not Bali Hai, because the naval guns had flattened every stick of paradise that ever existed there.

Since the planes had not yet arrived, some of us were assigned to burial duty. Not many Marines had been killed, but those who were had to be laid to rest. It was difficult to dig holes in coral, and it wasn't easy to carry a dead Marine in a stretcher to a boat that would take him to the next island, where the cemetery was located. I didn't know any of the men I was burying, and I tried to think of something else when I was carrying them.

The corpses were heavy and the flies were everywhere. Our burial detail was frightened and angry.

"Watch out where you're going."

"Don't worry about me, just worry about yourself."

"You're going to drop the son of a bitch."

"I don't need you to tell me I'm going to drop the SOB."

"You men shut the hell up and put that body on the boat. The chaplain has to say prayers and get back to his ship." It went like this all day long.

"Dead Marine coming through."

"This guy has no dog tags."

"Put him over there. You others look for his dog tags. I'm not burying any unidentified Marines. Washington goes ape when we can't identify the dead."

My only experience with dead people had been when I had delivered flowers to the funerals in New York. But those bodies were neat and clean. The Marine dead had not been prepared for burial. I got the willies when I put one on a stretcher. I wore a handkerchief over my nose, because the smell was awful. As I struggled with the stretchers, I said to myself, I wish I had sprays of fresh flowers to put on each one.

Burial duty is probably as rotten a detail as you can get in wartime. It isn't Taps and it isn't Arlington Cemetery. In World War II, it meant burying your dead on the spot, and then when the war was over finding a permanent home for the soldiers in a military or family burial ground.

Occasionally, I cried as I was carrying a body, as much because he was my age as because he was a Marine. Also he was so damned far from home.

While we tried to give some dignity to our own dead, we dealt with the Japanese bodies quite differently. Hundreds were loaded on dump trucks and driven to pits, where they were bulldozed into holes as just so much landfill. When the hole was filled, the dozers covered it without fanfare.

This was not retaliation. They had to be buried immediately because of the danger of a half dozen diseases spreading from the bloated corpses. There was no time for ceremony, as there had been several thousand defenders on Engebi and not more than two dozen had surrendered. The rest chose to defend the island in the name of the emperor, even if it meant trying to do enormous harm to us.

Staff Sergeant Tim Clark, who had also been on Guadalcanal, told us the Japs preferred to die in battle than be captured because it assured them a place in heaven. We were constantly told that a good Jap was a dead one. I am not a Japanese-basher, but the year was 1944, decades before I had any idea the Japanese would provide us with Toyotas, Hondas, and 26-inch color television sets.

More than half the equipment in my house is Japanese-made. If Tokyo had only explained to us in those days that all they wanted to do was sell us cars and electronics, I'm sure that we could have saved both sides a lot of money and ammunition. Nobody could have imagined that someday our children would be walking around with Sony Walkmans attached to their ears.

Our mission as a fighter squadron was to keep watch on islands that the Navy had bypassed on its way to Tokyo. The strategy was to neutralize the Japanese by bombing them every time they stuck their heads out of the ground. Our target was Ponape, a beautiful island which would have been too expensive to take, but was quite inexpensive to keep quiet.

That was the squadron's role. Mine was to clean guns and planes and edit a mimeographed newsletter called "The U-Man Comedy." It contained news of the squadron, which had been called the Whistling Devils—the name Tokyo Rose gave us. It was better than anything we could come up with. The paper even boasted poems—I wrote all of them.

The Ballad of VMF 113

Listen my children and you will hear
Of a squadron once quartered here.
Long ago in the age of jive.
Many a man is now alive
Who remembers these lads with fear.

★ ★ ★

Oh 113 was a squadron bold
Made from the devil's own brew.
The hell they raised shan't be forgot
Nor the hell that they went through.

* * *

Hush little children don't be afraid
They left by the dawn's early light.
Pray for the Jap that meets up with them.
I tremble to think of the sight.

Maybe it's not Kipling, but it sure raised morale in our squadron.

"The U-Man Comedy" was between two and four pages and, along with squadron news, had intermittent jokes such as: "Reporter to VMF 113 Fighter pilot: Were there any women on Engebi?—Pilot: Yes, there was one, but she died and some sentimental son of a bitch buried her."

I'll tell you what a tough editor I was. In one edition, I wrote an open letter to Tojo. Our squadron had shot down nine planes in one mission and on the front page I let Tojo know who did it. I described the battle in detail and then told him that it was time to throw in the towel. Even William Randolph Hearst never treated an adversary with such venom.

War for most men is not fighting or marching in parades. It is sitting around somewhere wondering what the hell you are supposed to be doing.

One night we were in a group drinking a homemade brew called raisin jack. West, who was from Tennessee, and played the guitar, said, "This island is worse than any outhouse in Tennessee."

Bowditch, our squadron philosopher, stood up and said after several tin cups of the home brew, "Do you know what war isn't? It isn't fighting for your country or your mother or the girl next door. War is sweating and freezing and defecating and eating and living too close to other men, and talking and dreaming and arguing and wishing you could get into some action, and be killed by something besides jungle rot. That's why I wouldn't mind being shot by the enemy. It still makes more sense than sitting around with you losers."

Engebi was a coral island surrounded by a sea of boredom. We were bombed once by the Japanese on March 8, 1944, and it would not have been too bad except the pilot got lucky and hit an ammunition dump. Everything from rockets to gasoline went flying, causing a fire one hundred feet in the air. We had all dug foxholes and that's where I was hunched over. I recall yelling at a tentmate named Farhart, "If there are no atheists in foxholes, what the hell are you doing here?"

I had my first real taste of fear that night and it remained with me for months. After that incident, every time there was an air raid drill I shook with fright, and crouched in a fetal position, and said things like, "I don't want to die." For the enlisted men of VMF 113, this was as rough as it could get. We lost some good pilots, mainly to bad weather. That mission in which our flyers shot down nine Zeroes made everyone feel good. But even better news came from Hollywood that Shirley Temple had agreed to be our squadron's mascot.

We passed the rest of the time on Engebi by going crazy. Our tents weren't too comfortable, so we had to scrounge for the wooden floors. The Seabees stocked up on wood, so we went out at night and "borrowed" whatever we could from them. The sailors let out a hue and a cry about this, even though we usually got along well. But flooring was in short supply and their orders were that our tents did not rate a high enough priority number, as compared to an officers' club. I made a scouting mission one moonless night in a stolen ordnance truck, and brought back enough lumber for a deck and an extra supply of two-by-fours to raise our tent off the ground.

The next morning, I announced that we had to lay the floor before the Seabees launched a search.

Carroll replied, "No way. Bob Hope is coming today and we're going to see the show."

I said angrily, "Look, I got the lumber—you guys have to fix the tent."

Cook said, "We haven't seen a woman in real life for a hundred years and the tent can wait."

I stood at the front flap. "Anyone who prefers Bob Hope to a floor has to answer to me," I declared.

My tentmates surrounded me with fists clenched. I sized up the situation and said, "Okay, I'll go see Bob Hope, too."

Years later, I traveled with Hope when he gave a show in Morocco, and told him the story. He said, "Your buddies were right."

Besides stealing lumber, we built windmills with plungers and cut gasoline drums in half. When the windmill turned, the plunger at the end rose up and down in the water and washed our clothes. I'm not certain who invented this machine, but it worked as well as a Whirlpool.

The enlisted men and the officers were separated by a coral path. The officers were a great deal more spirited than we were, mainly because they had bonded whiskey and had been issued pistols. Their flying skills were beyond question. On the ground it was another matter. Almost every night, the lieutenants got drunk and went outside of their tents to fire their guns at the moon.

For recreation the enlisted men brewed their own moonshine, the raisin jack I mentioned before. The beverage was produced by good old Southern boys who mixed fermented raisins, yeast, and sugar, and left it in pots and jars until the smell was so offensive you knew it must be time to drink it. The boys from below the Mason-Dixon line were the only ones who could sense the exact minute when the brew was ready. It had something to do with the rumbling sound the mixture made. If prepared properly, it tasted like Sears-Roebuck paint remover. On some enchanted evenings you could walk through our area and hear the rumble of the raisin jack coming from every foxhole. It sounded like Colonel Bogey's March.

One day, the Army colonel, who was commander of the island, walked through the area and found several stills. He only discovered them after he heard the noise. He ordered all of them destroyed.

When the word went out, our tent dug a second foxhole in the back, out of sight. Alas, this one smelled so bad and made so much noise that it was discovered in no time, and as punishment we were sentenced to heavy longshoremen detail, which meant unloading ships that anchored in the lagoon.

Altman was pissed. "We should have never built a still so close to our tent."

Carroll said, "Instead of trying to make it, why don't we buy some from Ackerman's still?"

West protested, "Ackerman's from Hollywood. He don't know nothing about making raisin jack. His tastes like ten-day-old rainwater."

A few days later, we were in the bowels of a landing craft, unloading a large supply ship, and were about to return to shore when the Captain yelled from the bridge, "I also have a motorcycle for the CO of the island." We waited in our landing barge for the crane to lower the net with the motorcycle in it. The net slipped and the crate came crashing down. We all jumped out of the way, and the box hit the deck and splintered into a thousand pieces.

Sometimes what it says on the container is not necessarily what's inside. The crate didn't contain a motorcycle; instead it was filled with cans of ham, chicken, turkeys, and everything Engebi residents would kill for. We hastily threw a tarpaulin over it. The captain shouted, "Everything all right?"

"The motorcycle looks as good as new, sir."

At gunpoint, we requested our bosun to take the landing boat in to a covet where we stored faulty ammunition. He did it reluctantly. We unloaded all the goodies into the stacked ammunition crates and then returned to the dock.

An aide to the commanding colonel looked at the manifest and said, "Where's the motorcycle?"

"We didn't see any motorcycle."

The aide was furious. He stared in disbelief at the mother ship as it steamed out of the lagoon.

After we got back to the tent, Brinkerhoff pulled out a letter he had found enclosed in the crate and read it to us.

"Dear Harry, Here is the Thanksgiving dinner we promised you and your staff. We hope you enjoy it and that everything is okay in the Marshalls. You're doing a great job." It was signed "Fishbait."

"God damn," Carroll said. "I remember 'Down and Out' Fishbait from the Point. He never forgot his upperclassmen. GO ARMY GO!"

I said, "Fishbait will be surprised to know how many people ate his motorcycle."

At that moment, four Army MPs crashed into the tent and searched it from top to bottom. They found nothing, and as they left, the soldier commanding the party said, "You gyrenes are going to be sorry."

As soon as the search party left, we sent word to the officers' club that we were willing to trade hams, turkeys, and chickens for sealed bottles of bonded whiskey. The response was overwhelming, and before the week was out we had a case of Old Grand-Dad and enough ham and turkey left to have a festive dinner in the tradition of military officers' clubs all over the world. We were feeling no pain when we got to the dessert, which turned out to be canned pumpkin pie and pistachio nuts.

Schmidt said, "We're selfish people. We're only thinking of ourselves. Why don't we send the colonel a turkey sandwich?" I wrote on a piece of paper: "Dear Colonel, The troops on Engebi love you very much because you never eat until your men are fed first."

The sandwich was made, the note was inserted, and I was dispatched to the colonel's quarters. You must understand that the colonel was a dogface, and the Marines did not believe he was protected by the rules of the Geneva Convention. I staggered to his tent, put the sandwich on his steps, and shouted, "Hey, Colonel, here is your effing Thanksgiving dinner." Then I took off like a gazelle back to Marine territory.

One of our extracurricular activities was to peddle "Jap" souvenirs to the merchant ships and naval crews that anchored in our lagoon. The most popular item was Japanese flags, which we made ourselves. We sprinkled red paint to resemble blood on the flags next to the Rising Sun. We charged anywhere from fifty to one hundred dollars for one, and I wouldn't be surprised if they are still hanging in the basements of ex-GIs as the proud souvenirs of World War II.

The sales were made from our landing craft, which cruised around the ships with half-naked men waving the flags in the manner of island traders.

We had many fistfights on Engebi, mostly out of boredom. They erupted over anything. One of my best pals was William Brinkerhoff. He had a very pretty girl back home and carried her picture everywhere. One day he received a letter from his mother, telling him that his girl had been seen dating other guys. He asked me what I thought.

"Maybe your mother is lying."

"Don't you call my mother a liar," he yelled, and then started swinging at me. For an hour, we lunged at each other. We finally quit when I said that his mother wasn't a liar and his girl wasn't doing what his mother claimed she was.

I often found myself in fistfights over my Jewish persuasion. A few of the men in our squadron had problems with Jews, either because they had never met any, or because there were not many Jews in the Marine Corps. Once you were called a dirty Jew, or even just a Jew, you had no choice but to fight, or risk being considered a Jewish coward. I wasn't big and I wasn't strong, and I wasn't even bar mitzvahed, but when someone challenged me for being Jewish, adrenaline surged through my body, and I just kept swinging with tears in my eyes.

I can't tell you how exhausting it is to continually defend all the Chosen People. The anti-Semitism I experienced was mild, if you don't include the time Fedlock broke my thumb because he said I had killed Christ.

Since I was young and cocky, I wasn't sure whether my fights with other Marines were because they thought I was a little shit, or because I was Jewish. Like most Jews I always assumed that the only reason anyone picked on me was that they were anti-Semitic.

In the beginning, I fought all the time but after a while I realized that it wasn't getting me anywhere, so when someone insulted me, I just said, "Stuff you" and I walked away.

At our VMF 113 reunion in 1991, I asked Sully if he was aware of any antipathy toward Jews. He said, "Once, when I promoted you to sergeant, one of the men in ordnance came up to me and said, 'How can you promote a kike before you promoted me?' "

At the same reunion, Sully related a story to me that I had forgotten. One day at El Toro, we were lined up at attention facing three Naval chaplains across a large empty hangar.

An officer yelled directions, "All those of the Catholic faith, go to that area. All those of the Protestant faith, go the center over there." The ranks had thinned out to me. Finally, he said, "And all those of the Jewish faith, go to that area."

Sully said, "You were the only one to walk to the Jewish chaplain. I thought to myself, 'That's the longest walk I've ever seen any man take.' "

Because so many of the guys in my outfit had never met any Jews before, they just didn't know how to behave around one. Some of the men from small towns tried to be nice to me by telling me that they knew a Jewish family named Kaplan or Leibowitz where they came from—and grew up playing with their kids. The family usually owned the store in town and were "as nice as they could be."

My response was, "I am very happy to hear that. If you run into the Kaplans, be sure and give them my regards."

While I was battling to defend my people, my father's Jewish acquaintances at home were telling him that anyone who joined the Marines was a crazy mixed-up kid who didn't have a brain in his head.

I continued to have run-ins with Marines who didn't like me for whatever reason. I was happy-go-lucky, and that didn't go over too well with some men who were lacking humor and who couldn't understand what I had to be happy about.

Sully was kind and gentle and a superb non-commissioned officer, and he still is a friend. At the reunion, I asked him what he remembered about me.

He replied, "We used to call you little Artie in those days. You had the ability to screw up a two-car funeral. Anything you touched ceased to function.

"None of my section leaders wanted you on their plane crews. As soon as you were assigned to one, the guns would start to jam or the fuses on the bombs would fail to go off. It wasn't that you didn't try. You just weren't born to be an ordnance man. You were born without an ounce of mechanical ability.

"I really didn't know what to do with you, because you were a willing worker and always anxious to please. So I came up with a job for you. I assigned you to drive our bomb truck loaded with munitions to the line. It was the perfect job, because you would have no one breathing down your neck and you had to report only to me.

"I took you behind the ordnance tent," Sully continued, "and gave you the keys to the truck. Then you got a funny look on your face and said, 'Sully, I have never driven anything in my life.'

"That's when I really got mad at you and said, 'Well, goddammit, this is as good a time to learn as any.' And I threw the keys at you."

"Do you remember how I did as a truck driver?"

"You had a few misses with the bombs in the back of the truck, but I don't think you hit anything."

When I look back, I'm not unhappy that I didn't have what it takes to be a good ordnance man. It must have been the God of Abraham who kept me from being able to load a .50 caliber machine gun. Had I been successful, I might have chosen to stay in the Marine Corps and been assigned to deliver atomic weapons in my bomb truck.

On Engebi we harpooned sharks, found cat's-eye shells in the water, played volleyball, and saw an occasional movie. It wasn't much of a war, but I had learned after Parris Island that the secret to a long life was to keep my mouth shut and never, ever volunteer for a better assignment. Since the Marines have a purpose for everything and were in charge of my fate, there was no reason for me to change their game plan.

I asked Sullivan at the same reunion why he thought we were all so close still and had such warm feelings for one another.

He replied, "Because we compressed a lifetime into a few years and we experienced things together that no one else will ever share. Today they call it bonding. Some people might call it love."

One day, a ship anchored offshore and unloaded a fresh group of enlisted men. It turned out they had come to relieve us. No one was made more welcome. We gave them our windmill washing machines and sold our "Jap" souvenir flags to them at cost.

The next stop for the squadron was Okinawa, where the new men saw far too much action from kamikaze planes. Again I was saved by someone at Marine headquarters who was looking after my best interests. At the beginning of the war, I was sorry I couldn't find some real action. Now I accept the fact that being relieved by the new recruits was another piece of luck which guaranteed my survival.

Finally the big day came. We were told we were going home. Our troopship was old and slow. No one lagged behind when we boarded. For the first time in over a year, our bow was pointing in the right direction. It took us thirty days to get to San Francisco.

One footnote: When we left the island of Engebi, we all assumed that it was the last we would ever hear of it. But this was not to be. Engebi became part of the H-bomb tests after the war. They wired the island with every conceivable atomic device available and then someone pushed a button and blew it sky-high. I'm told that it doesn't exist anymore. Others say it exists, but only rats can live on it.

When I read about the test, I wrote a column pointing out that the scientific data from the blast could be faulty. The explosion may not have been made by atomic bombs at all, but rather by our raisin jack that was still buried in the coral. Any scientist who ever tasted it will swear our homemade brew was far more powerful than the plutonium warheads.

The trip back to the States was wonderful. I played chess every day with a fellow I didn't know. We never exchanged names. We just set up the board every morning and went at it. On the last day we didn't even say good-bye.

In Hawaii our ship was tied up next to Hickham Field's officers' club. Except for the women in Bob Hope's troupe, the beautiful ladies going in and out of the club were the first we had seen in over a year. We all hung over the rail, whistling and cheering them. There were so many troops on board that the ship started to tilt to starboard, so a worried captain divided us into A and B watches and allotted fifteen minutes of ogling before we returned to the port side of the ship.

It went like this. Over the loudspeaker, "Watch A to port, Watch B to starboard. Fifteen minutes."

The most amazing part about this was that the watches did

as they were instructed. I was Watch B and as I headed for the rail to stare, the men going to the other side muttered to us, "We saw three gorgeous blondes enter with one pathetic dog-face officer."

I remember another saying to me, "Watch as they get out of their cars. Their skirts go up to their thighs as they get out." I stood at the rail, squinting as hard as I could and thinking, "There isn't a bad one in the bunch."

We studied and discussed the shapes of the women and for the first time in centuries it dawned on us that perhaps there was more to life than killing sharks and digging coral out from between our toes.

Anyone who tells you that the Golden Gate Bridge is the most beautiful sight in the world as you approach from the Pacific is right. We sailed under it and broke into song—and continued singing for several hours.

By the time we unloaded at Treasure Island, it was midnight. There were two or three thousand of us and a few started yelling—nothing you could understand—just yelling. This was picked up by others, until three thousand voices were yelling or groaning and moaning. Lights were turned on and people rushed to their windows. Those in charge of us pretended they didn't hear anything, because they knew it would be suicide to stop us.

That night I was assigned a bunk, and I flopped in it dead tired. In the morning, instead of a loud wakeup call I heard a flute over the loudspeaker, followed by a string quartet playing classical music.

"Oh Christ," I said, "I'm dead."

I checked with squadron mates and they all thought the same thing.

It seems that the receiving officers at Treasure Island wanted to make our lives as pleasant as possible and told a staff member who had been stationed in heaven to draw up the plan.

We were issued new uniforms. Despite all we had done to win the war, we were entitled to only a few combat ribbons. I was in the PX looking into a glass case that displayed the ones which fighting men had earned when Sully walked by and said, "Buchwald, get your ass away from that counter."

I made one dumb blunder when I arrived at Treasure Island—I rushed to the telegraph office and sent a wire to the Markays notifying them that I had just landed in the United States. I thought that they would be pleased. But the telegram was delivered at two o'clock in the morning. Western Union was in charge of notifying loved ones of casualties and deaths in the armed forces, and when Mrs. Markay saw the delivery boy at the front door, she fainted. Bob, her son, was fighting in Europe with the 1st Division, and she was certain that the telegram was about him.

Finally, and with great ado, I was ready to go home—the son of John Wayne, a child of Montezuma, foster child of Corporal Pete Bonardi.

It was the best time for a Marine to return to the States, since there was a shortage of Marines who had seen combat, and we were very much in demand for dances, social life, and moonlight romance.

The beauty of being a U.S. Marine during World War II was that when someone saw you in uniform they never asked what you did in the war. They assumed that you were either at Guadalcanal or Iwo Jima. I never once lied or exaggerated my role in the hostilities. It was done for me by people who wanted to believe that I was a hero. Protesting their assumptions did no good, because the more I denied it the more modesty they thought I showed.

I had no choice but to relax and enjoy it.

I boarded a train with a couple of men from the squadron—Dumbarton and Ruggeroni. We sat in seats facing each other, with a stranger occupying the fourth one. He kept eyeing us. Finally, he said, "You guys must have been through hell."

We didn't know what to say.

"You don't have to talk about it if you don't want to," he continued. "How many bastards did you kill?"

Dumbarton said, "We never counted."

"If it hadn't been for a bum football knee, I would have been with you."

"We could have used you," I said.

"How many guys did you lose?"

Ruggeroni said, "We never reveal our casualties."

Two civilians sitting behind us leaned over. One said, "My brother's a Marine."

The other one added, "I have two nephews in the Navy."

"The Navy has a lot of good people," I told him.

The stranger said, "If you guys ever want a good steak in Oklahoma City, call me." He handed us his business card.

The whole scene was getting a bit much, until Ruggeroni looked up at the ceiling and said in a loud voice, "Listen. I heard them. They're Jap Betsies. Everyone take cover." He dropped to his knees.

He then yelled, "Bogey at four o'clock. Zeroes coming in from the West. Fire one, fire two. Oh God, they hit the mess hall."

The strangers moved away from us, and suddenly everyone pretended that we didn't exist. Ruggeroni climbed back into his seat, winked at us, and then fell asleep.

We made it to Grand Central Station without any more questions.

I was both excited to be home and scared silly. Most of my life I had been leaving home, and now I was coming back to it. I had fantasized so much about this moment when I was overseas that I knew it couldn't possibly live up to my expectations.

I wanted Forest Hills to be exactly the same as when I had left it. Everything was supposed to be frozen in time. It didn't turn out that way. The shops were the same and the buildings were as I remembered them, but all the people I knew were different—I was different. For one thing, all my growing up had taken place in the Marines. I was very sure of myself. I had been tested (not as much as I pretended) by my stay in the Pacific and all my other adventures in the service.

I came out of the subway station with my seabag, and arrived at the apartment house. The same doorman was manning the foyer. His only remark was, "Long time no see."

The family knew that I was in the States but they didn't know when I was coming. So it was a surprise when I showed up at the door around eight o'clock at night.

Doris was away in the Army, but Edith and Alice and Pop were home. There was a lot of screaming, shouting, and hugging. Everyone was talking at once. Edith kept squeezing all the parts of my body to make sure that I wasn't wounded. Alice immediately started fixing a hot meal, and Pop had a big grin on his face.

The girls were grown up, too. Pop hadn't changed that much. He seemed genuinely glad to see me, and for all of us the moment of reunion was one of celebration.

I thought to myself, "At least they're not pissed off at me."

In an hour, however, things began to deteriorate. I found myself getting itchy and bored. I didn't have too much to say, other than how glad I was to be home, and they were afraid anything they might say would offend me.

I announced that I was going out to visit friends. What I did was go out and get drunk.

I met another Marine in a bar who said, "Eleanor Roosevelt has put out the word that Marines, having tasted blood, are coming home like killers, and she has recommended that we be re-educated in camps so we can become normal human beings again."

"No wonder people have been looking at me oddly. I notice that everyone is nervous around me. All I have to do is belch and someone brings me an Alka Seltzer," I said.

One of the first things I wanted to do was go back to Hollis and revisit the places where I had spent my childhood. Hollis had left a far greater mark on me than Forest Hills. I rode out in a cab and picked up Milton Stevens, then home on leave from the Army, and Warren Cooper, who had served in the Navy. The three of us marched down Hillside Avenue like a Camel cigarette advertisement.

One of our P.S. 35 playmates, Harvey Carlson, had been killed at the Battle of the Bulge. He had been drafted and had had less than eight weeks of training before they sent him over. Of all the gang, Harvey was the brightest, and his loss was a terrible waste.

We knocked on the door, and Mrs. Carlson answered it. Harvey's father was sitting in the living room. Mrs. Carlson knew us well and made us hot chocolate.

"You look nice," Mr. Carlson said.

No one knew what to say. Finally I blurted out, "Harvey was a great guy."

Milton said, "It shouldn't have happened."

Suddenly, everyone in the room was crying. It's one thing

to see a person you served with get killed in battle; it's another to share the death of a boy you grew up with. He was our age, our friend, and someone of enormous promise. Harvey's death affected me as much as anyone's I had witnessed in the service.

After a few days at home, I felt uncomfortable. Everyone seemed like a stranger and my family still treated me like a child. I missed the men of VMF 113—they were the only ones I was close to in my teens.

Whenever I wanted to relate a funny story about the Pacific, Edith would say, "Don't talk about it."

Alice was still concerned with the details of how I had run away to join the military.

Today the runaway story has become legend in the family, and I retell it with the same gusto that someone recites *A Christmas Carol.* My nieces and nephews love it, and my sisters only interject when their roles appear in the tale. The part people seem to enjoy the most is when I tell them about Flossie and the University of North Carolina in Greensboro.

As Edith said, "I always suspected that he was going to do something like that."

Alice told me, "The FBI wouldn't even help us."

Edith added, "Pop never slept one night."

A few days after I came home, Edith hit me with an unexpected question, "Arthur, are you married?"

I was floored by the query. "Hell, no. Why do you ask?"

She whipped out a photo of Gwen, her one-year-old son Al, and me on the beach in Santa Monica. Edith had found it among my belongings in the foot locker I sent home.

"That's Gwen," I said. "She is a widow friend of mine and that's her son, Al."

Now it was Alice's turn. "Are you going to marry her?"

"I don't think so. At least that wasn't exactly what either of us had in mind."

Edith said, "You should be ashamed of yourself. You took advantage of her."

"How do you know?"

She slapped the photo. "It's all over the picture."

Then it dawned on me what they were driving at. "I'm not the father of her child. His father was killed in a RCAF training mission."

Edith asked, "How old is she?"

"I don't know. What's going on here? I've been in the Pacific. You have no right to dictate who I can or cannot go out with. Furthermore, if I did want to marry her, I would. I've always been attracted to older women with one-year-old sons."

Then the final question from Alice: "Is she Jewish?"

These were the kinds of conversations I was having at home. Pop was glad that I was alive and well, but we didn't have those talks in the library between fathers and sons that they showed in Andy Hardy. Maybe it was because we didn't have a library.

At the time, Uncle Oscar owned a bar in Brooklyn which was located in an area noted for Murder Inc. Most of the clients were gentlemen who never took their hats off.

I went to visit Oscar. When I walked in, several of the customers eyed my green uniform. Finally, one of them asked, "Hey, are you a customs officer?"

"No," I said, "I'm a Marine."

His companion said, "You could have fooled me."

Oscar came out of the back room and said, "This is my nephew."

That made me all right and pretty soon everyone was offering to buy me Scotch or sell me a crate of stolen cigarettes.

Oscar had nothing to do with these people, other than to sell them drinks. He was always trying to make a financial killing, but he just didn't have the knack. He bought the bar from another man without checking out what kind of clientele patronized it. He aimed to please his customers, which meant having to purchase everything on the black market, leaving little profit for himself. Eventually, he lost the place and all his money.

Although no one talked much about it, the black market in New York seemed to be one of the city's major businesses. Everybody knew somebody who, for a price, could get you anything you wanted. The main reason that so many people gave for dealing with the black market was that everyone else was doing it.

The conversation went like this. "You're a brave man and I want to do something for you. I can get you a good portable typewriter for $150."

Kremshin down in Bensonhurst was the main source of rubber tires, and Bugle in the Bronx had all the silk stockings.

During my time away, Aunt Rose had moved into the same apartment house as Pop and the girls, and she was truly happy to see me. Her son, Carlton, was flying B-17s over Tokyo, and Leonard was an officer in the Navy. Since I had lived with her for so long, she was not only fond of me, she thought of me as her third son.

She had become very disturbed over the fact that several times I appeared at her apartment drunk. She had never seen me like that and assumed that the war had turned me into an alcoholic.

It hadn't. I never really liked the taste of liquor, and I may have been drinking because that's what Marines were supposed to be doing when they were home on leave. I always pretended that I was much drunker than I really was, because liquor made me sleepy. I also behaved silly. Once, I was in the famed Copacabana, I was drunk, and I ran into Leonard, Aunt Rose's son. He was home on leave and was sitting with a pretty girl. "Hi, Leonard," I yelled. Leonard was embarrassed and said, "Karen, this is my friend, Arthur."

"Friend!" I screamed. "I'm his damn cousin." Leonard didn't even ask me to sit down, but he told his mother about it the next day.

I found more interesting companionship in bars. Another reason that I drank so much was that everyone in New York insisted on buying me free drinks. I noted that as soon as I was out of uniform and had to pay my own bar bills, my alcohol consumption dropped down to almost zero.

The home leave went by. I, of course, was hoping that as a Pacific hero, I could find a girl who would hold me in her arms and tell me how grateful she was that I had kept her from being ravaged by the Japs. But it never happened.

Once a girl handed me her telephone number on the subway, but I was afraid that she might have a husband who would beat the hell out of me.

Doris Augustine, from my days at Forest Hills High School, called and invited me over to her house. No one was home, and after a few minutes of sparring—"What ever happened to Al Holzman?" and "Do you ever hear from Gloria Clinton?"—we clinched and our tongues met.

I thought, "This is it. This is what I waited two years on Eniwetok for."

But Gloria backed away. "I don't want to," she told me.

"Why not?"

"You're too nice."

"I'm not that nice," I protested. "I can be a real rotten person when I want to."

"I want to be your friend," Gloria insisted.

"I am your friend, but even friends can get in the sack once in a while."

She started to cry and that was it. What made me mad was that when I eventually returned to Cherry Point for duty, everyone claimed that they had to beat their women off with broomsticks.

The three weeks were up and it was time to leave. I wasn't upset. I had lost all touch with civilian life and my nest was now in the Marine Corps. Everyone's big fear, including mine, was that I would be sent back overseas for a second tour of duty. It didn't appeal to me or to any other member of my family, but I had no say in the matter. It was a ribbon clerk in Washington who would decide my fate—that and Harry Truman's decision to drop the bomb.

I was relieved to be back in Cherry Point, where I was assigned to torpedo school in Jacksonville, Florida. Someone at Marine Corps headquarters reasoned that since I didn't know anything about bombs there was no reason I should know anything about torpedoes. It was a three-month course, and the only plus for me was that Jacksonville was a slightly better liberty town than Cherry Point.

I graduated with honors in torpedoes, but the Allies can thank their lucky stars that I never had to set one for firing, or I would have sunk our own ships. Following Jacksonville, I was given a leave home.

Then the most unbelievable event happened. I was in New York City on VJ day. No one can imagine what it was like to be a Marine on VJ night in New York City. People hugged me, girls kissed me—my hand was sore from being shaken. Then I went and did something stupid. I bought a pint of very bad whiskey called "America the Brave." It was even worse than raisin jack. I drank the whole bottle in four minutes and proceeded to get sick on the curb at Broadway and 47th Street. I presented an awful picture, a disgrace to my uniform, my country, and to the Great White Way. Why, on this night of all nights, I chose to get drunk instead of enjoying the moment is something I have often asked myself, since I could have been dancing in the streets with a Rockette from Radio City in my arms, or a Smith girl like the ones I used to ogle at the Biltmore. I could have been taken to the Stork Club by a divorcée whose boyfriend was a lieutenant on a destroyer off the Philippines. I could have wound up seated on a couch in Frank Sinatra's dressing room at the Paramount Theater. Instead, I put a dagger in my stomach with a pint of the worst rotgut money could buy. For once, the God of Abraham wasn't there when I needed him. On the other hand, he must have had a lot more important things to do on VJ night than to worry about a drunken Marine.

I did wind up in someone's bed on the West Side—alone. A Puerto Rican lady had taken me home and put me on her couch. "America the Brave" blew my head off, and the hangover was worse than anything I had suffered during World War II. The lady made me breakfast, and I rode the subway grimly back to Forest Hills.

The war was over and the powers in charge decided that the Marines would be released from the service on a points system. That meant that those who had seen the most combat were to be discharged first. I had no quarrel with that. What made it difficult was that the Marines had no idea what to do with the rest of us.

So at Cherry Point they turned us over to a sadist—Master Sergeant Twofang Whip (not his real name). His qualifications for treating men as human beings came from the time he had been a prison guard at Sing Sing—I am not making this up. Sergeant Whip sent us out every morning to cut down trees, dig holes in the roads, and then fill them in. Except for lacking dogs, we could easily have been members of a chain gang.

We were permitted to talk, and the main conversation was how we could kill Whip and still receive a Good Conduct Medal.

One afternoon I was walking past the athletic field and stopped to watch the Cherry Point football team in practice. Then an idea hit me. I went up to a man who looked like the coach and said, "Sir, do you have a publicity man for the team?"

He said that he didn't.

"Well," I told him, "that used to be my racket before the war. I worked for Paramount Pictures in their publicity department. I'd like to let the world know what a wonderful team Cherry Point has."

He said, "We probably could use you. What do you want me to do?"

"Just write a note saying you need me very badly." (Father Murphy would have been proud of me.) The coach wrote a note which I produced at next morning's roll call. I could tell Whip was pissed off because he would have one less man to carry rocks from one side of the road to the other.

But I was joyous.

I started interviewing the players and upgrading their biographies. For example, a tackle who played one year at Marquette was described in my press release as "A former All-American star who had shot down five Zeroes and would probably be drafted by the Chicago Bears after his discharge." A running back from the University of Montana had broken the conference record for touchdowns in one season before he became a war hero in the Pacific, by throwing himself on a hand grenade.

Every player in my book was a Medal of Honor star athlete, and the coach was the Marine's answer to Knute Rockne.

For the record, the Cherry Point football players were a sad sack of potatoes, who were either mostly over the hill, or too young to know where the hill was. But publicizing them was a living.

One day I was ordered to appear in front of the colonel in charge of Special Services. He was grim. "Sergeant, be prepared to leave for Washington in one hour. We're flying you up by Torpedo bomber."

"Is it all right to ask why, sir?"

"Cherry Point has a game with the Air Transport Command, and now that the war is over, Washington would like to make sure that the Marines put on a good show. We want the Cherry Point name plastered all over that town. This thing comes down from the top."

The orders were fine with me, and before I knew it I was on my way to Washington with my press releases and photographs.

When we landed, I was met by a Marine chauffeur, who drove me to Marine Corps headquarters, where a female master sergeant was waiting to take me down long halls with mysterious designations on office doors such as "NewCom," "DayPac," and "BackPac."

I was hoping to meet the Marine in charge of personnel who had been so nice to me with my assignments and thank him personally for giving me such a good war.

We arrived at a large office with double doors and the stars of a general emblazoned on them. I walked right past the secretaries into a room filled with a couple of generals and God knows how many colonels.

I stood at rigid attention.

"Relax, sergeant," someone said.

I wanted to retort, "Are you out of your mind?" Instead I just stood there like ice.

"Sergeant, now the war is over we must beat the U.S. Air Transport Command. Can we do it?"

I looked at the grim faces staring at me and shouted, "YES, SIR."

The General asked, "Does Cherry Point have a good team?"

"They're Marines, sir. They don't know what losing is."

The brass was very pleased with that reply.

"If we were to bet, could we spot them ten points?"

"I would spot them fourteen," I said.

A colonel said, "Then fourteen points it is. Now you understand, sergeant, that in peacetime, sports plays a significant role in how the public perceives the services. We're counting on you to ensure that we'll be playing a real ball game."

I drew myself back to attention, "You can count on me."

When I left the office, I was introduced to a tall gangling Air Force first lieutenant in the anteroom. It turned out that he was one of seven public relations personnel representing the Air Transport team. When he discovered that I was the only PR man assigned to the Cherry Point squad, he was overjoyed.

"Come over to the Shoreham," he said. "We're having a party."

"What about whipping up interest in the game?" I said.

He took my press releases and my photographs and said, "Don't worry. We'll handle that."

He wasn't lying. There was a party and it lasted for four days. People kept coming in and going out—I never got anyone's name. There were girls and officers and there was liquor and there was room service. We were prepared to fight the Japanese for four more years.

Occasionally, I would read the sports pages. They were full of stories about the Air Transport Command. One of them ended with, "They will be playing the Cherry Point Marines."

The Marine brass was also reading the sports pages. In less than two days, an all-points bulletin was sent out for Press Agent Sergeant Buchwald. When they found me, I was told to report pronto if not sooner to headquarters.

The colonel in charge of keeping the generals happy read me the riot act. He had the newspapers spread out on his desk. He couldn't believe that we were losing the battle of the press releases.

"Sir, I've been saving our ammunition for the last four days. That's when it really counts."

"You better be right."

It was time to make the rounds of the newspapers. I told all the editors the same story. I was outnumbered and outflanked by a vicious Air Transport press machine. My career in the Marine Corps would be finished if I failed to get a story and a photo in the papers. If Cherry Point did not receive due recognition in the next few days, I would be sentenced to guard duty in the Aleutian Islands. I told the tough sportswriters that they were my only hope. They were moved.

No one turned me down. They tore up sports pages to print pictures of our players. They described our line as the seven blocks of granite—Marine players who had honed their skills on Saipan and Peleliu, men who were trained to tear the Air Force into pieces.

Our running backs were depicted as superstars who were dying to show the pro football scouts what they could do. Their whole futures depended on this game.

It was stuff that football hype is made of, and no one could complain that I wasn't doing my job.

The game was set for Sunday. The team arrived in town on Saturday. I greeted them at the bus station. They were happy to see me. "Where's the party tonight?" one of them asked.

I said, foolishly, "You have a game tomorrow. You can't party."

One of the tackles lifted me off the ground.

"We want to go to a party."

"Of course you do," I said. "And I know some people who would be very happy to have you. If you put me down, I'll make a telephone call."

Our social gathering was as good a party as anyone attended in World War II. Women from all over Washington volunteered to act as hostesses. Members of the team drank themselves under the table.

It lasted until it was time for the team to go on the field. The coach, who had been up all night himself with a female Marine officer, showed up and looked at his players and said, "Oh my God."

I still remember the stroll I took past the boxes in Griffith Stadium, where the top officers of Marine headquarters were seated with their wives waiting for the Cherry Point leathernecks to kick the living daylights out of the Air Transport Command. Several of them waved to me and made the victory sign.

I made the V sign back, just like Winston Churchill would have done.

The game was a rout. The Cherry Point players kept falling down and refusing to get up. The ball fell out of the hands of the running backs over and over again. For most of the game, I just stared at the ground. The final score was something like 48 to 0.

After it was over and no one was talking to each other, I said to the coach, "What should I do now?"

"You better stay around and clean things up."

"I think I ought to tell you something," I said. And then I told him the entire story of my arrival in Washington and my visit to headquarters.

He heard me out and then said, "On second thought, you better come back with us."

Two weeks later, a grim Special Services colonel called me in and asked, "How would you like to get out of the Marines?"

"I don't have enough points."

"Don't worry about that," he said. "And don't ask any questions."

And that is how I was honorably discharged from World War II on November 12, 1945, by a grateful Marine Corps.

It was an unforgettable day for me. I had survived the toughest things Tojo could throw at me without a scratch. If a gypsy had looked at my palm, she would have predicted that I would have a wonderful future ahead of me. I had almost forgotten Flossie, who was responsible for my joining the Marines in the first place.

The importance of those three years' service was that they were the ones that would have caused me the most trouble if I had remained in civilian life.

I owe the Corps a lot. When I meet another Marine, we share a bond. It's like belonging to the same lodge.

This illustrates how strong the bond is. A few years ago I was speaking at a college, and a very pretty girl was assigned as my escort. She told me her father was a Marine colonel serving President Nixon, who was then in retirement at San Clemente.

The next morning she was giggling and said she had called her father, who was very embittered at the media, and said, "Dad, guess who I am escorting around campus?" When she told him, he said, "That SOB." Then she told him, "But Dad, he was a Marine." Her father responded, "That's the only good thing about him."

I used to tell Marine stories to my children and at dinner parties, but then I noticed their eyes glazed over. I discovered over the years that the only one who will listen to your stories is another Marine, on condition that you listen to his.

I can now say without hesitation the Marine Corps was the best foster home I ever had.

10

USC

I hadn't given much thought to what I would do with my life once I was discharged. I was in love with Southern California and my only plan was to become a famous screenwriter and make love to Ginger Rogers. Little did I realize that there was no such thing as a famous screenwriter in Hollywood. There are rich ones who make thousands of dollars and play tennis every morning and lunch with their agents in Bel Air—but no one knows their names.

I assumed that with my mail room connections, I would have no problem being hired by the studios at Paramount Pictures to write movie scripts for Bob Hope and Bing Crosby. The only two things I wanted very badly were a screen credit and a tennis court in my backyard.

I also gave some thought to education. Three years at Forest Hills High School without a diploma didn't seem like enough credentials to persuade anyone that I could be a writer. My plan was to go to high school at night and make up credits, get a diploma of some sort, and then enroll in college. It wasn't all that clear in my head at the time, but you could call it my ballpark thinking.

My farewell from the Marines was filled with as much serendipity as my entrance into it from Greensboro. I had to get from the East Coast to the West Coast, and I really didn't want to pay the fare. So although I had been discharged (they gave us a ruptured duck to wear on our uniforms for thirty days), I put my uniform back on and hitchhiked to Washington from New York. I then proceeded to Anacostia Field, an air base for the Naval Transport Command. Their job was to move people in and out of Washington, to and from every part of the globe. A nice WAVE put me on a passenger list for a plane going to San Diego. I offered to buy her dinner, which she was happy to accept. It was over spaghetti and meatballs that I became cocky and told her I had already been discharged from the service. She panicked and ran out without finishing her dinner and immediately took me off the passenger list.

So I found myself at eleven o'clock at night, sitting in the waiting room at Anacostia, trying to figure out what made me tell the WAVE that I was no longer in the service. Then I wandered to the window and saw a beautiful Liberator bomber on the runway. I asked a Navy clerk who it belonged to.

"Admiral Jocko Clark. He's a war hero."

"Where is it going?"

"San Francisco. That's his pilot over there."

I went over to a Naval commander. "Any chance of bumming a ride with you?" I said. "My brother just got back from the Philippines and he's in the hospital with malaria. I don't think he's going to make it."

I know Marines are not supposed to tell lies, but the war

was over, and I could always blame my fibbery on the Pacific coral that was still stuck between my toes.

The pilot said, "It's okay with me, if the admiral doesn't have any objections."

I sat with the crew and we waited until three o'clock in the morning for Jocko to show up. When he did, he was with a woman, who really did look like Rita Hayworth, and he was kissing her good-bye and wouldn't let go of her ass—and she was trying to tear off his epaulets. The pilot shook his head and said to me, "The hell with it—get on board."

I sat in a seat in the back trying to remain as inconspicuous as possible, at least until we were airborne. Finally, after take-off, a Navy steward came up to me and said, "Can I fix up a berth for you?"

I played it cool. "That would be very nice."

In a few moments, I was in heaven—flying across the United States in my own berth on an admiral's plane. It seemed just the right way for a GI to return to civilian life.

The next morning, I had breakfast with a very hungover Jocko Clark. I didn't want to talk too much about my combat experiences, so I asked him about his. He had no idea what I was doing on his plane—but he assumed that I had to have done something really brave to rate a ride with him.

The admiral acknowledged my salute as we deplaned, and we both wished each other well. I was tempted to ask him about the beauty in Anacostia, but I decided it wasn't such a great idea.

From San Francisco, I hitchhiked to Beverly Hills. I had no idea what I was going to do. My first step was to look for a place to live. I went to the Hollywood Canteen, where I had spent many evenings in the past. They had file cards on people renting rooms and I took one that sounded interesting. It was located on Sunset Boulevard and cost twenty-five dollars a week with breakfast and dinner.

The place was a replica of a Normandy castle and rose in splendor on a hill overlooking Los Angeles.

It had an imposing doorway made of impregnable wood that would have stopped Ben Hur. The lady who answered the bell was forbidding. One side of her face was all scaled, and she seemed unable to smile.

I showed her the file card and she let me in and took me to the room. It was large and had two beds and she said I had to share it with another gentleman. The dining room seated twenty people. As far as I was concerned, it was a perfect place and I gave her my rent in advance.

One of my first discoveries about my roommate was that he was a set designer and he was gay, which didn't bother me one way or the other. But he used this awful perfume, which was so strong it kept me awake at night, and he was unimpressed that I had been a Marine. He also made no attempt to hide the fact that he didn't like me.

The dining room was wonderful. Thirteen or fourteen of the most beautiful girls I had ever seen were living in the house and taking their meals with me. They told me that they were all starlets waiting for their big chance. Every once in a while, a long limousine would pull up in the driveway, and one of the girls would leave the table and disappear into the night.

While they were civil to me, I couldn't connect with any of them. I claimed to be a screenwriter who was working on a hot property for Paramount Pictures. I let on that my story was about a little boy who was kidnapped in France by his beautiful nanny and brought to the United States. It would need a certain type of actress to play the little boy's nanny—and then I would give a description quite similar to whichever girl I was talking to.

It didn't work. I spent most of my evenings reading books and smelling cheap eau de cologne.

After a week, I decided that I wasn't having any fun and I would find a new place to stay. I left without anyone saying good-bye to me, and I walked down the long hill to the bus stop. A man waiting for a bus said, "How is it up there?"

"It's not terrific."

"Are you kidding? That's the greatest call house in America."

I was genuinely shocked. I looked back at the house and said, "Now you tell me."

"Yup. They charge one hundred dollars a night and the limo is extra. Did they give you any samples?"

I grinned as if to say, "It's none of your business."

Then I asked him, "Why do they take in male boarders?"

"To make the place look like a legitimate lodging house. They pay off the police, but they still have to have an air of respectability."

Several months later, I read in the newspaper that the house had been raided and there were photographs in the paper of the madame and some of her girls being led away. I stopped regretting that I hadn't stayed.

It was time to face up to whether I was serious about attending school. My decision was to go down to the University of Southern California and find out what I should study at night to get into the place. There were at least 4,000 ex-GIs waiting to register. I stood in line with them. Hours later, I arrived at the counter and said, "I would like to . . ." The clerk said, "Fill this out."

"Yes, ma'am," I said.

"What do you want to take?"

"It doesn't matter."

"Math?"

"Sure."

"English?"

"Why not?"

"History?"

"Of course."

"Have it stamped over there."

A man stamped it and I was in college.

It was a miracle.

As soon as I was accepted I wrote to my sisters.

Dear Alice, Doris, and Edith:

I know this will come as a terrible shock to you, but I've enrolled as a student at the University of Southern California, which was my first choice. Actually, it was the only school I applied to.

They didn't bother to ask me about high school credits, assuming that no one would apply without a high school diploma—unless he was going out for the football team.

All your predictions about what would happen to me if I goofed off in high school have not proven to be true. USC sees something in me that you girls never did—a promising brain surgeon, a future member of the Supreme Court or, at the very least, a Nobel laureate in literature.

No doubt in the future someone at the school will discover that I dropped out of Forest Hills, but by then it will be too late to do anything about it. I am determined to maintain a B average and become the manager of the school's rowing team.

I have never been happier in my life. As soon as I mail this letter I am going out to buy saddle shoes and get a date with a Trojan coed—Jewish, of course.

Tell Pop he can start sending me salami again.

Love,
Art

Like all my dreams that came true, getting into USC was one of the turning points in my life. It gave me a home after the Marine Corps. I had no idea why I was going there—certainly not for a degree. But, once enrolled, I was able to postpone decisions about my future.

This move also gave pleasure to my father and the girls. They could brag about me to their friends without worrying about me getting killed.

The decision to go to California meant that I had left their home for good. I don't know if, subconsciously, I wanted to be far, far from the area of my childhood, but California was a new beginning. From then on, I became an infrequent visitor to Forest Hills. It no longer held any ties for me.

I never missed it. My memories of Forest Hills were that the apartment was too small, that I had no space or privacy. Someone was always asking me what I was doing and where I was going, and when I was coming home. The family setup was stifling me—I knew I could never live there again. And I never did.

Having been accepted as a full-time student under the GI Bill, I was entitled to seventy-five dollars a month plus tuition, books, and supplies. It was perfect, but sure enough, a year after I enrolled, they called me in and said, "You don't have a high school diploma."

"I know," I said.

"Then you're not supposed to be in college."

"I know. What do you want me to do now?"

"We'll make you a special student."

"What does that mean?"

"You can't work for a degree."

"I don't care about that. I don't have a high school diploma—so there is no sense having a college degree."

Meanwhile, I found a boardinghouse a few blocks from school, run by a cheery little woman who was like a mother to her thirteen boarders. While she liked us very much, she hated blacks, Jews, Hispanics, Orientals, and other minorities—not necessarily in that order. She used to subscribe to a weekly German newspaper with a swastika on the front page. I saw it in her living room when I went to pay my rent. Mrs. Liebschen did not connect her tenants with the races and nationalities she despised. We had a communal kitchen off our bedroom on the second floor. We wrote our names on the packages of food we kept in the icebox. We didn't have any say about who our housemates would be, but we got along very well. My first roommate, Birmingham, was not serious about studying, and a few weeks after school began, he was arrested for sticking up a grocery store. He disappeared, and was replaced by Bill Lyle, who was unarmed and wanted to be a dentist.

At that time, just after the Second World War had ended, an undeclared class war was going on at USC. The GIs returning home had little use for the fraternity men, since most of the frat boys were not only much younger, but considered very immature.

The GIs were intent on getting their educations and starting new lives. Some fraternity people partied, drank, cheated on tests, and tried to take over school politics. In those days, the administration catered to the fraternities, knowing that eventually they would be the big financial supporters of the school, as opposed to the independents, who would probably not be heard from again.

I lined up with the independents. I did publicity for Jesse Unruh, who later became a power in the California legislature. I also wrote liberal articles in the newspapers and made fun of the Greek system.

It wasn't my first decision to favor the have-nots over the haves. I had been doing it all my life, and I confess that it may have had something to do with my envy of the haves, starting with their Christmas trees and girlfriends under the clock in the Biltmore.

A lot of it revolved around symbols. I used to make fun of kids who lived in nice houses and rode bicycles and who seemingly had no trouble making the football team.

The Marine Corps class system—officers vs. enlisted men—was a little easier to accept, because the division of the two groups was presumably based on talent rather than money.

But USC was the perfect place to decry the inequity of the system—of which I felt a victim. In the Student Union one day I declared that all people who owned convertibles were airheads, except coeds whose fathers had given them to the girls as presents and couldn't help themselves. I also declared that Greek fraternity men lost one million brain cells an hour from the sun beating down on their heads while they were surfing.

I have made a good living making fun of people who had more possessions than I did. USC was my training ground before I went out into the world and stuck pins into the rich and powerful. What a joy it was in later life to get paid for the things I was always mad at.

Years later I discovered the real extent of the school's support of the fraternity system when I challenged Walter Wanger, the producer of *Joan of Arc,* to a duel in Paris because he hadn't liked my review of his film. The challenge made headlines all over the world and a reporter from the *Los Angeles Times* went to the USC Alumni Office and asked what kind of student I had been. The official he talked to said, "He was even a Communist in those days."

Another source they looked up was an English professor named Frank Baxter. Professor Baxter became famous as the Shakespeare guru of television. I had taken a course in humor from him. It wasn't hard. All we had to do was laugh at Baxter's jokes. The only paper we were required to write was on what we got out of the course. I wrote "NOTHING"—which was my joke. I wanted to test his humor. He gave me a D, which I now brag about on television talk shows.

When the reporter interviewed him about it, he said, "Buchwald and his class were a bunch of imps, leprechauns, catalyzers, delights. It was a yeasty bunch. He did not bother to be a good student. He got what he wanted from us and I don't think he took anything he didn't want."

He was certainly right about that. When it came to extracurricular activities, I was at the top of my form. When it came to studies and grades, I was the bottom of the heap. Creative writing courses excited me—foreign languages and the sciences interested me as much as nuclear waste.

The main thing USC did was to give me an opportunity to write. I had a great time as managing editor of the *Wampus,* the school humor magazine, with my pal Al Hix, the editor, and I loved doing a column for the *Daily Trojan.* I took playwriting in the drama department, creative writing in the English department, and courses involving various forms of literature. Because I liked what I was doing, I behaved myself in class. When I took a course I hated, I reverted to being the class clown.

I am partial to students who rock the boat. Some years ago I established a scholarship at the school of journalism at USC for the most irreverent student. I stipulated that he or she had to be first and foremost a good writer. But outside of that the winner did not have to toe the line as a student. I said that if the person was on probation, it was in his favor. The winner didn't have to thank me and I, in turn, didn't have to find the student a job.

There have been seven winners so far. They have all lived up to my expectations. One recent recipient sent me a card from Capri, which said, "I just thought you would like to know what I did with your money."

The business manager of the *Wampus* was a young man named David Wolper.

He had nerve and imagination. He would call up the studios and talk them into having Jane Russell and Sophia Loren photographed reading the *Wampus* magazine. He took women on summer vacations across state lines for illicit purposes and promised to make them Hollywood stars.

David and I spent a great deal of time together. We attended a nudist camp, professing to be true believers in bare skin and diving into the swimming pool every time we got an erection.

Then there were the receipts from the *Wampus.* They were brought to us by beautiful coeds who sold the magazines on campus.

We spread the dollar bills out on the desk and counted them as follows, "One dollar for the school, one dollar for us, one dollar for the school, one dollar for us."

One day in 1948, I asked Wolper, "What do you intend to do when you get out of here?"

He said, "Television is getting big. They have no film because no one will sell them any. I'm going to start a company and find them programs. I don't care if it's about lawn mowing or VD. The stations are going to have to buy them."

He was as good as his word and started a company called Flamingo Films. Then he sold it and incorporated another one called David Wolper Films. He must have sold his company a couple of hundred times and made money whenever he did it. Among his accomplishments, he produced *The Race for Space, The Making of the President,* and *Roots.* He also went on to stage the entertainment side of the Summer Olympics in Los Angeles and the New York harbor gala celebrating the 100th Anniversary of the Statue of Liberty in 1986.

But I like to think that I was involved in his greatest triumph.

When I was in Europe I worked on a documentary about the manufacture of Belgian shotguns. After writing the English script, the Belgians asked me to sell it for them. I wired Wolper from Brussels.

"Have tied up exclusive American rights to Belgian shotgun flick. Will let you have it for 200 dollars."

In typical Wolper fashion, he cabled back, "Will pay 100." I made the deal and that shotgun picture played every TV station in the United States—in prime time. I still get royalty checks of $1.60, so even now it's showing somewhere.

David and I keep in touch. He is constantly being honored

at some fund raiser and he always suggests to the sponsor that I would be happy to speak about him for nothing.

Wolper was also the publicity man on a varsity show I wrote called *No Love Atoll.* I collaborated on the show with a friend from my boardinghouse, Ray Pippin. The storyline of the musical concerned an island similar to Bikini which the Navy had selected for nuclear experiments. The job of the Naval destroyer was to remove the islanders, first by diplomacy and then by force. In the end the islanders persuaded the crew of the destroyer to stay. It was topical, to say the least.

I consider Wolper's work as the show's PR man one of his earliest triumphs. He hired a limousine and rented a gorilla costume from Western Costume. David stuck a friend in the gorilla suit and I sat on one side and he sat on the other, and the chauffeur drove us up to the Shrine Auditorium, where they were holding the Academy Awards.

The doorman opened our door, and the three of us got out. We walked straight down the red carpet into the theater. On the back of the gorilla, it said, "If you think this is great you should see *No Love Atoll.*" They had no idea what was going on and we walked up and down the aisles for twenty minutes before the show started. Finally, they threw us out, but the stunt worked and we made the pages of the papers the next morning.

Another idea David concocted to call attention to our show was to keep planting stories in the paper that a South Pacific expert was coming to the school to lecture on the native inhabitants of the atolls. David brought a young man on campus in a grass skirt and bare feet. His first words were, "Shit on all people who live in Pasadena."

When the show played at Bovard Auditorium, people were

impressed. One of the actors in the cast had an uncle who was a big chief at MCA, then a vast talent agency handling everyone from Clark Gable to Ronald Reagan. It also had a large literary department. The hope was that MCA would represent the show and sell it to the movies.

Several weeks after sending the script over, I was given an appointment to see Mr. Burp. I went to Beverly Hills with high expectations. On the bus, I planned my negotiating strategy. I was going to insist on writing the movie script myself. The company would have to pay for the idea and also the script. I would keep all book and foreign rights. They could take it or leave it.

I sat across from Mr. Burp, looking very cool. He was about to say something when his phone rang. I listened in on the conversation. "The new Irwin Shaw book is better than *War and Peace*. It's called *The Young Lions* and we're starting at a million dollars. I'll let you read the galleys, but I want them back tomorrow morning. You better act fast, because six studios want the property. Right. Get back to me, but don't try to bargain."

Mr. Burp picked up my script and looked over at me and said, "As for you—get this piece of crap out of here."

On the bus going back to school, I thought, "Maybe I was too tough."

During this period, I continued to write to my family in Forest Hills. My sisters were tremendously relieved that I was attending college, although they were surprised that the school had let me in.

I wrote to Doris:

I'm having a ball. I wear a cotton sweater that could be taken for cashmere, and nobody gives me a bad time or tells me what to do. Actually, I am the envy of many of my friends because I am not working for a degree and can take any subjects I want to.

When asked what I intend to do with my life, I reply, "I'll probably be a writer for the cinema, or start a book on the corrupt athletic programs in our university system. I'm talking to several publishers right now."

Guess what? I'm living in a boarding house with thirteen other guys. I am very comfortable because our foster child background was wonderful training for living with thirteen slobs.

I am very popular spinning tales of those days because it was an entirely different childhood from the ones any of them had.

Tell Pop that the government sends me an allowance every month so I am eating just fine. He doesn't have to worry about coming to my graduation because I'm not going to have one.

I know that you are now a nurse in Brooklyn Jewish. I'm glad no one at Brooklyn Jewish realizes how close to danger they really are.

Love,
Art

A highlight of my college experience did not take place at USC, but in the summer of 1946 when I was on vacation. I went north for work and wound up in a town called Marysville. It was fruit-picking country, and I yearned to live the life of a sharecropper and write a sequel to John Steinbeck's *The Grapes of Wrath.*

I got in line with many down-and-out people and felt very proud to be among them. A man with a clipboard walked up and down inspecting us. "We're picking grapes," he said.

"I gotcha," I said thinking of *The Grapes of Wrath.* He looked me up and down to make sure I didn't have TB and then said, "Get on the effing truck." About thirty of us piled on, most unshaven, unbathed, and a few hostile and dangerous. We went off to the fruit ranch. As we unloaded, I noticed a few sinister things—all the gate keepers had shotguns and the people in charge of us were armed with truncheons. We were told that we had agreed to work for a week, and anybody who tried to escape would be filled with buckshot.

The barracks were intimidating. There were bunk beds—the mattresses were stained and filled with straw. Not since my first night at the Hebrew Orphan Asylum had I been as frightened. I could smell cheap liquor, and I could hear loud snoring and coughing, and the cries of men having nightmares. People were getting up all night to go to the toilet.

I wondered if Steinbeck had ever spent a night in a place like this.

I said to the man who had a bunk under me, "I don't like this place."

"It doesn't matter if you do or not. You're stuck for a week. They would keep you a year if they could. What do you usually do for a living?"

I said, "I'm a college student."

"Oh my God, and you come here to write a paper on us."

"No," I protested. "I was really looking for work. I'm flat busted."

"If they find out you're a college kid, they'll beat the hell out of you, because they'll suspect you of being a union organizer. Don't tell anyone else what you do on the outside."

"I get you," I said. "Is the work hard?"

"It'll break your back."

I had taken on more than I could handle. Many of the people in the dormitory had hit the bottom of the barrel or were illegal immigrants. My bunkmate pointed out a few Mexican workers and told me to stay away from them because they carried sharp knives and would use them on anybody's lower parts.

I was unable to relate to anyone in the barracks. I also knew that whatever their story was, I couldn't write it. The way I felt, I couldn't even write *Of Mice and Men.*

Sleepless and shaking, the next morning I ate a breakfast of gruel and coffee and went out into the fields to pick grapes. After four hours my back ached and my eyes hurt from the sun. *Grapes of Wrath* or no *Grapes of Wrath,* I had to get out.

I planned to make a break for it as soon as I could. A few days later, after my back was in agony and every muscle was sore, I made my decision—I was going to go over or under the fence.

At midnight I went out to the gate. I told the guard I had just seen two men go over the fence and he rushed after them with the dogs. I walked out the gate and then ran as hard as I could for as long as I could—the sound of hounds barking in the distance made me break every migrant mile record in the book. I didn't look back. That night, I slept in a field and vowed not to become a writer about people who made their living off the land. I didn't even write a paper about it for school.

I have had nightmares over the years—the worst ones during my depressions. Among the pictures I see in the nightmares are those of the barracks in Marysville, where I watch men in their tortured sleep snoring and coughing and muttering to themselves.

The vision of being trapped behind barbed wire, sleeping with sick and dangerous strangers, and getting up at five o'clock in the morning to pick fruit is my idea of what hell must be like.

The fact that I had thoughts about Marysville when I was suicidal was an indication of how serious a scar it had left on me. When my depression was at its deepest, my psychiatrist was perplexed when I kept talking about having to go out and pick grapes. It took a while before he realized that I had actually done it.

From Marysville, I headed east to Lake Tahoe, hoping to land a job at a gambling casino. The lake straddles two states—California and Nevada. The gambling all took place on the Nevada side. There were not too many casinos at that time—one was called State Line, another was Cal Neva. Cal Neva, which required black tie of its customers, had dozens of men in tuxedos with bulges on their chests—bulges caused by what could easily be described as cannons. The big stars played there and, except for an occasional disagreement concerning a person's gambling losses, it was considered the safest casino on the lake.

I applied for a job at a place called Tahoe Village—a new casino rumored to have been built with bricks reserved for a housing project for the poor in Reno. In those days, building materials were rationed and only available for homes and apartments. As a result, the black market came into play when the owners constructed their casino. They gave shelter to more people than any other structure on the lake, they maintained—when those people were gambling.

It was an impressive rotunda building, and out front it

featured a thirty-foot neon sign of a cowboy who constantly kept drawing his gun and firing it off and then putting it back in his holster.

I asked to see the manager and volunteered my services in any capacity. He said he had no jobs. I noticed the manager's boots were very dusty, so I said, "Do you have anyone to shine shoes?"

He said he didn't—so I talked him into letting me be the shoeshine boy for the casino in exchange for room and board. It wasn't much of a job, but everyone from the owner to the bellboys came to see me twice a day.

One evening as I was shining the owner's shoes, I said, "You don't have very good publicity around here."

"What do you know about it?"

"That's really my racket. I just shine shoes because I can't find a publicity job."

"What would you do if you ran the publicity department?"

"For starters, I'd give away free breakfasts on Sunday morning. What have you got to lose?"

The owner thought that it was a great idea—and the next Sunday, the place was jammed with freeloaders who couldn't pass up a free meal.

The result of the breakfast idea was that I was promoted from shoeshine boy to publicity director.

I was a success. When the owners and manager weren't there, they put me in charge. One time, a busboy came yelling that the chef and the maître d'hôtel were chasing each other with knives and were prepared to hack each other up.

I rushed into the kitchen and shouted, "Knock it off."

The chef stopped in his tracks and said, "What goes on? One day you're shining my shoes and the next day you're telling me to knock it off."

There was something incongruous about coming from the fruit-picking stalag at Marysville to the gambling world of Lake Tahoe. As much as I hated the whole idea of how the growers collected their food, at least they were providing a needed commodity for the nation's tables.

The casinos, on the other hand, sucked up people's money and gave nothing back. I used to count the winnings from each table early in the mornings and I knew how weighted the odds were in favor of the house. The whole thing was so dumb, because people were willing to lose their life's savings for a free breakfast.

One day, I was wandering around the casino and I stopped to watch the craps table. A man who looked like my father was rolling the dice. He must have had three thousand dollars in front of him. I thought of Pop struggling to make a few bucks and getting deeper and deeper into debt—in a legitimate business—and I was turned off by the whole gambling scene. Since then, I've played poker and gin rummy for very small stakes, but I have never thought of big-time gambling as an answer to my financial problems.

In the two months of working at Tahoe Village, I witnessed loser after loser being issued bus tickets back to where they wanted to go. The clients weren't any use to us anymore, and if we got them out of the area, we wouldn't have to look at their pathetic faces.

While I was there, I met a girl. She was a blackjack dealer at the State Line Casino and very attractive. I think she thought that since I wore a shirt and tie at night, I was a big shot at Tahoe Village. I encouraged her to think this. We used to take long walks along the lake in the afternoon. She said that she wanted out of the gambling business, but the money was too good, particularly the tips, and she couldn't afford to quit.

I told her that although I had a piece of the action in the casino (lies, lies, lies), I really wanted to be a writer and possibly publish a novel based on a beautiful girl like her, trapped in a den of greed by gangsters and people who didn't pay their full share of taxes.

Although we knew each other's secrets, we never made it to the sack. She let me understand that I could sleep with her, but her hours were so weird—from eight in the evening to three in the morning—and I could never stay awake long enough. A few times, I actually slept in her room waiting for her, but I was so groggy when she arrived that I just said good night and went home.

I liked her very much because she was sad and vulnerable and she felt trapped. I was sure that someday she would appear as a character in one of my screenplays.

At the end of the summer, the owners asked me to stay on, offering me one hundred dollars a week plus room and board. It was a lot of money and guaranteed me a future. But something told me to get the hell out of there. It may have been the easy money, the smell of greed, or the fact that none of the ways they earned their living made much sense. I said I would come back after I finished school.

I never had to, because a few months later one of the owners shot the other in a dispute over the way one of them was dividing the profits.

By this time, I was certain I wanted to be a writer, and therefore any adventures such as Tahoe were good experiences for my chosen career.

One adventure I enjoyed took place when I became a salesman for a roofing and siding company. I was hitchhiking on Olympic Boulevard when a fellow named Johnny G. picked me up. He said he sold siding, and if I worked with him I could make a lot of money in my spare time. Everybody in Los Angeles needed roofing, siding, or a barbecue pit, and the Bank of America would finance anything the homeowner wanted.

He told me that I didn't have to make the sale. All I had to do was ring the doorbells and get the residents to agree to see Johnny. My sales pitch was that I was from the Glutz and Freebone advertising agency and we were looking for a house in the neighborhood on which to advertise our new Johns Mansville all-weather, fireproof aluminum roof. If my advertising manager selected their house, they would be given a roof at cost. When someone asked the homeowner where they got the roof, they would get a ten percent commission for referring a new customer to the agency.

It was a straightforward proposition, Johnny said, and one that would make me rich.

I tried it. I worked a neighborhood with a big fat guy named Pedro. I rang bells on one side of the street and Pedro rang them on the other. Every once in a while, he would disappear into a house and I'd have to wait for thirty minutes on the corner.

Then he'd come out zipping up his fly.

"She was a very nice lady." Pedro smiled. "Very *simpático.* She didn't need a roof, but she needed much loving."

"You screwed her?" I yelled in disbelief.

He shrugged his shoulders. "She was very lonely."

I pounded on his chest. "How did you know?"

"I always know."

"Look," I said, "I have an idea. Tomorrow I'll work this side of the street and you work the other side."

"All right."

The next day I rang bells furiously and waited for the magic moment. It never happened. In the meantime, Pedro continued to disappear into houses and invariably came out grinning.

He said, "I spoke to her husband in the office and he agreed that they needed siding. She would not let go of me while I talked to him. It was nice for both of us. I also sold him a barbecue pit."

Sadly, this was an experience I never shared with him. All that happened to me was that one day an old man answered the door with a fiddle in his hand and invited me in. He had no furniture in the living room and asked me to sit on a wooden crate. Then he started to play for me—for two hours. I never thought that I'd get out. When I did, Pedro was waiting for me, drinking a Coke. "So how was it?" he asked, assuming I was having a fling.

"Great," I said. "We made music for two hours."

Years later, I found out that the guys in the siding and roofing business were known as suede shoe boys. They weren't crooked, but they also weren't members of the Mormon Church.

Once I was hanging around the office on a Saturday afternoon when a lady called in and complained that no one had taken a picture of her roof for advertising purposes. The boss said, "That's a terrible omission. We'll send our man over right away." He threw a Brownie camera at me and said, "Go to this address and take pictures."

I told him, "There is no film in the camera."

He said, "Get out of here."

Johnny G. had a sense of humor. Every time he sold a couple a roof, he demanded that they produce a Bible and put their hands on it and swear they hadn't lied to him.

I made a few bucks with Johnny and it was a great education, but after Pedro's experiences I couldn't keep my mind on my work.

So I gave up the business and opened my own advertising agency to service two accounts. One was Eddie's Oasis, an off-campus student bar, and the other was the Allied Surplus Company, which specialized in war surplus material. In order to collect fifteen percent commission on the ads for my clients, I had my own letterhead printed to bill the school publications. Naturally, I called my company "The Art Buchwald Advertising Agency," so that there wouldn't be any doubt about who owned it.

I wrote copy for both Eddie's and Allied and I also bought space in the *Wampus* to place them. So I had the best of both worlds and so did the humor magazine.

I held one more job that might put me in the Hall of Fame for television pioneers. In 1947 while hitchhiking, I was picked up by a man named Johnny Parsons, who identified himself as the West Coast sales manager for Philco radio. At that time, Philco was also producing a limited number of television sets.

Johnny was stationed in San Francisco and was slightly hyper. He was a promoter in the true sense of the word and was constantly thinking up stunts. He asked me if I wanted to be his man in Southern California for fifty dollars a week. I accepted.

The job consisted of attending shows at KTLA and reporting back to Johnny on their quality. This wasn't hard, because no one had a TV set and I certainly had no idea what was good and what was bad.

The second part of the job required my attendance at the Los Angeles Dons football games (they belonged to a league that no longer exists). I was to arrange the commercials for Philco radios. This is what I did: I handed a portable radio to a group of fans in their seats. Then I signaled the cameraman, who zeroed in on the people as they listened to their radio. A voice in the studio would read the copy, and then when it was over I'd grab or wrestle the radio away from the fans and place it in another part of the stadium.

I carried the portable to all four sections of the Coliseum. It may not have been the first commercial on TV in Los Angeles, but it was without doubt the cheapest one.

From Marysville to Lake Tahoe, the real world made itself felt during the summer, and even when I returned to school, it continued to intrude in various, uncomfortable ways. Things were changing in the country, and not always favorably.

I used to hang out at Actors' Lab, which was located behind Schwab's Drug Store on Sunset Boulevard. I hoped to meet important people or aspiring starlets there who were in search of young writers with whom to share their milk shakes.

One day, I saw a sign on the bulletin board which said, "Come to Dalton Trumbo's House to Free Poland. Everyone Invited"—then it gave the address in Beverly Hills and the time.

I couldn't believe it. Trumbo's book, *Johnny Got His Gun,* was one of my all-time favorites. It was the antiwar novel of the decade and it stayed with me and haunted me. Trumbo was inviting me to his house. I got all dressed up and arrived on the dot. When I met Trumbo, I told him he was the greatest writer in the English language. He shook my hand weakly and indicated where the bar was.

I wandered around, rubbing shoulders with guests who I assumed were the outstanding movie makers of our time. One couple started speaking to me and we became very friendly, particularly when they discovered I went to USC. "What do you do?" they wanted to know.

"I'm a writer," I said. "I write books and short stories and movie scripts."

They said it sounded as if I had a great deal of talent.

"My professors seem to think so. But I'm not selling out. If I write a movie script, I want complete control or it's no deal. I didn't fight the Japs in the Pacific to sell out at home."

When I told them I was a columnist on the school paper and worked on the humor magazine, they were even more impressed. They invited me to dinner at their house on Sunday night to "discuss my career."

We didn't have more time to speak, because people started to make impassioned speeches about Poland. I'm not certain what side they were on, but everything said at the party was tilted toward Eastern Europe and away from the United States. Whenever the brave Russians were mentioned, there was applause. I have no idea whether anybody in the room was Communist or not, but they liked Moscow a lot more than I did.

Of course I kept these thoughts to myself, because I didn't want to get bounced out of Trumbo's house. I was only interested in talking about the movie business, but they all wanted to talk about Warsaw.

The dinner date with the couple I met at Trumbo's took place the next Sunday, but it was not what I expected. I brought along some stories I had written, but no one bothered to open the envelope.

There were only four people besides myself, and the conversation went something like this:

"Would you consider USC a reactionary school?"

"Probably," I replied. "But I have no idea what a reactionary school is."

"Do you know if there are any Socialists there?"

"I know of two. They're brothers and they are real dyed-in-the-wool screwballs."

"Have you ever read Karl Marx?"

"No, not even for Civilization 103, when it was required reading."

"Would you consider starting a Writers Club for us at USC?"

"Who is us?"

"The people who are working to advance the principles of good writing."

I suddenly got their drift. "Have you invited me to dinner to recruit me?"

"You could do a lot of good for Hollywood if you helped. Our finest writers came from the ranks of university students."

"I am not interested in recruiting anyone. All I want to do is become a rich screenwriter."

"You can become a fighter for democracy and be rich at the same time."

"Can I go now?"

"If you wish to, but think about our proposition."

"I'd love to, but I have an awfully heavy schedule as it is."

I left before dessert, because I was afraid that the FBI would crash into the house and arrest me as a co-conspirator.

As I departed, the host asked me, "Aren't you worried about Fascism?"

I replied, "I am, but I am much more worried about flunking medieval history."

It was my first taste of Hollywood and I often wonder if they found somebody else at USC who was more favorably disposed toward socialism.

While I have always professed to be a liberal, my credentials are spotty.

When I was younger, in order to prove that I was on the side of the underdog, and not prejudiced, I ate with the black kids in the cafeteria at Forest Hills High School. I thought that I was making an important statement. But before long I became the butt of all their jokes and they wouldn't stop needling me about being a "good white boy." They had seen through me, and I left their table and stopped being a friend to everyone regardless of race, creed, or color.

The Red Scare of the forties and fifties was really frightening in Hollywood—it was possibly the worst period the entertainment industry ever endured. The anti-Communist politicians shouted that the Reds had infiltrated all of show business and were going to destroy the country.

I didn't know too much about this until I went to Paris after USC. Many victims of McCarthy wound up there because they could not get work in the United States. My friends were Larry Adler, the harmonica player; Michael Wilson, who co-wrote *Bridge on the River Kwai* under a fictitious name; Jules Dassin, who made the classic *Never on Sunday* in Greece; John Barry, one of our finest American composers; and others who had refused to name names.

Since most of the blackballed people were talented, they were able to make a living in Europe.

I have always ridiculed the political extremes. I discovered that the right and left did not have a sense of humor. Besides, they were never willing to listen to another person's opinions on any subject.

As a child of Franklin Roosevelt I was interested in the

plight of poor people, had compassion for the minorities, believed in unions, eyed management of any kind with suspicion, and was certain that the power structure of the country was only out for itself.

I have never gotten over feelings of revulsion for what the Germans did during World War II, but I seem to have made my peace with the Japanese—to the point of owning a Japanese-made car.

Maybe it's because the Japanese didn't kill any Jews.

When I was at USC, I used to say that I was a Democrat with mixed emotions about Harry Truman. Most of all, I had a strong suspicion that the Communists, their sympathizers, the KKK, and the Commie-hunters were threats to me.

I was prepared to fight to the death for their right to believe what they did, but I secretly prayed they would all wind up with syphilis.

During those years at USC, I also had the occasional brush with anti-Semitism, but I only remember one incident clearly. There were the gentile fraternities and the Jewish ones. A student did not attempt to enter the other's turf. A friend of mine named Charley Peterson, who was on the staff of the *Daily Trojan,* was in one of the meanest fraternities on campus.

One day while drinking a lot of beer, Charley decided to pin me—which fraternity men do when promising fidelity to their women.

I kissed him and everyone in the bar cheered.

But the following Monday Charley was called on the carpet with some of his brothers—not for pinning a male, but for pinning a Jew.

Charley, who had a great sense of humor said, "I didn't know he was Jewish."

I am not one of those who is constantly looking for slights

against the Chosen People. I suffered no cruelty during my USC days. The school was mostly liberal and I don't think that it discriminated against us. As a matter of fact, not long ago the Jewish chaplain at USC, a lovely person, asked me to address a dinner for Jewish alumni. I asked her how many people she was contacting and she said, "I don't know, because we have no idea how many Jewish students attend the school."

"Why not?" I asked.

"Because when they enrolled, USC never asked them."

It's hard to imagine, but I had no love life all the time I was in college. The reason was that I couldn't afford one. Another was that sorority girls were difficult to date. With few exceptions, they only went out with fraternity men, which was a good idea since they had the money, the clothes, and the *savoir faire* which it took to be a success in Southern California.

I went out with several coeds but I never felt comfortable about it. My social life was confined to outsiders—mostly working girls who had nothing to do with USC. I met a nurse once on the beach and saw her a few times. On another occasion, I met a secretary who worked at Paramount Pictures. She was considerably older, which was just fine as far as we both were concerned.

I found that there were a lot more lonely people in Los Angeles than anyone imagined. I think that the reason I got along so well with the few women I dated there was that I had experienced terrible loneliness for most of my life and I knew exactly what was going on with them.

I managed to have fun in my own way. One time a friend of mine, Dixie Lee Turner, was dating a student named Joe

Large, and they wanted to go to Paris together. Dixie's father, who lived in Phoenix, was adamantly against it. I suggested that I write a letter to Mr. Turner, as the fictitious father of a girl named Sandy who would be accompanying Dixie.

Here is an excerpt from the letter:

> I am writing this letter to you because it seems we have something in common—both our daughters are determined to go to Paris. I have granted Sandy permission for the trip because I trust her with Dixie Lee. The French consul in New York is a family friend and he assures me that everything is just fine in Paris now. He told me that the consulate could arrange living arrangements for the girls and they would be properly chaperoned.

The rest of the letter continued in the same vein. I thought that it was very convincing but I failed. Mr. Turner smelled a rat and told Dixie that she would never go to Paris with Joe. Dixie said, "Sez who?" and went.

Joe and Dixie eventually married, but Mr. Turner mistrusted him so much that he didn't speak to him for ten years. I always thought my letter concerning the Paris trip had a lot to do with this.

Another time, Al Hix, my buddy from the *Wampus,* and I drove down to Tijuana, just over the Mexican border from San Diego. Tijuana was pretty raunchy in the forties. It had bars and it featured prostitution and other vices, such as X-rated live shows with the animal of your choice.

We had nothing in mind except to sightsee. Along the way, we stopped for beers. Al was the driver, so he had a lot more beers than I did. By the time we got to Tijuana, which was five o'clock in the morning, Al was blotto. He was the type of person who, when he got drunk, went into some sort of trance and had no idea what he was doing.

Just after we arrived, I was walking along the main street, which looked like a scene from a Western, when I turned around and saw Al in an argument with the driver of a small vegetable truck. It seemed that the motor had stopped and the driver was trying to repair it. Every time he touched an engine part, Al lifted the man's hand and shook his head. The driver was shouting and Al was shouting back, saying something like Mexicans didn't know a damn thing about cars. Before I could drag him away, two policemen arrived.

They grabbed Al and steered him toward the police station. I tried to persuade them to let me have him, but they wouldn't do it.

We marched in single file—policeman, Al, policeman, with the truck driver and me bringing up the rear. When we reached the station they threw Al into a cell and told me to get the hell out of there.

I went to have some breakfast and then returned to the station. I had seen enough movies to know that a person must always act with humility when talking to Mexican officials. I said to one who spoke a little English that I knew we had insulted the great country of Mexico and its truck drivers and I apologized on behalf of all tourists. I promised that I would take my friend to the border and he would never return to Mexico again. The Chief told a guard to bring Al in. The policeman shoved him onto a bench.

Al still had not sobered up. When he saw me, he said, "Listen, Buchwald, I want to be my own lawyer. These Mexes have no right to hold an American citizen and I want to talk to the American ambassador."

I said as calmly as I could in perfect English, "Keep your mouth shut, you asshole."

Then Al got up to leave and the chief yelled at him to sit down. Al said, "I have to go to the bathroom."

The guard laid a heavy hand on his shoulder and pushed him back down on the bench. The chief was agitated, and I made a desperate final pitch. "He's only a stupid college boy. He meant no harm."

I looked at Al to make my point, when I noticed a puddle of urine forming under the bench. The chief hadn't seen it and neither had the guard. Finally, the chief told me to get him out of there, and if he ever saw him in town again he would shoot him on sight. I dragged Al toward the door, while he kept shouting, "Leave me alone, Buchwald, I'll be my own defense."

I threw him in the car and got behind the wheel. As I was backing out, the chief and guards came out on the steps shouting at us to come back—the puddle had been discovered. I pretended I didn't see them. Now I have to tell you something. I am not a good driver, and in those days I was an even worse driver, but when we were leaving Mexico I drove better than Andretti. I was afraid the border police had been alerted, and while Al slept off his binge I perspired off five pounds.

When Hix woke up that evening in his house in Whittier, he had no memory of being in Tijuana, no memory of being in a police station, and no memory of sullying the chief's wooden floor. He claimed that I had concocted the whole story. What hurt even more was that he never even said, "You're a helluva driver."

The Mexican police wasn't my only close call. I almost got sucked into the Korean conflict.

I was walking on campus one day, and a student from my

history class said to me, "You were in the Marine Air, weren't you?"

"Yeah," I answered.

"Well, we have a reserve squadron out at Long Beach and you can make fifty dollars a month and we don't have any planes, so all you have to do for your money is play basketball."

That seemed like a good idea, and I told him I would go down with him the following Saturday.

When I got to the Long Beach Naval Station, they made me fill out papers and then they gave me a physical examination. I passed with flying colors. The last stop was the dentist's office. He looked in my mouth and said, "You have four cavities and we're not going to fill them. Come back when you get your teeth in order."

That really upset me. If they wouldn't fill my cavities, I didn't want to be in the reserves. I never went back. As soon as the Korean War started, the Marine squadron received its airplanes and in a month they were gone, flying over Inchon and a lot of other parallels. My rotten teeth had saved my life.

And that's the way it went for me at USC—a charmed life. Looking back, I can see lots of glorious hills and very few valleys. In fact, when the editor of this book first read about my experiences at USC, he became exasperated. He called me and said, "Didn't *anything* terrible happen to you in those days?"

I tried to think of something to please him, but if it did happen, it had left no scars.

"Look," I said, trying to reason with him. "If you had survived my childhood and the Marine Corps in World War II and you wound up in one of the leading universities in the country without a high school diploma, and nobody gave a damn if you got a college degree, and Uncle Sam presented you with a monthly check of seventy-five dollars, and Santa Monica was only thirty minutes away, and the sun shone 360 days a year, and there were no such things as drugs or campus violence—doesn't it figure that any person could have had a nice day?"

The nicest USC day of all was on May 7, 1993, thirty-seven years after the registrar told me I couldn't work for my degree. On that morning, I appeared on a dais in front of the Doheny Library, facing 32,000 people, and was awarded an Honorary Doctor of Letters. I was also the graduation speaker, and I told the students about my failure to get a diploma and pointed out that since USC had seen fit to give me a doctorate all these years later, all of them had wasted their time.

It was a very moving occasion for me, in the same class as the times I addressed the Hebrew Orphan Asylum and the University of North Carolina at Greensboro, Flossie's school.

As I sat on the stage, my mind wandered back to the school years—to a time when so many students returned from the war to begin their lives again.

From my seat on the dais, I could see Bovard Auditorium, where my varsity show, *No Love Atoll,* had been produced. Also within sight was the Student Union, where I had been managing editor of the *Wampus,* and written for the *Daily Trojan.*

I remembered the drama building where I had had a featured role in a play. I had acted the part of a Mexican and the *Daily Trojan* drama critic sarcastically said that I was another John Garfield. Then he beat the bejesus out of me. All this came flooding back to me so strong that I was afraid I might cry. I longed for all the people I had known at USC to be at this graduation and sit there with their mouths wide open as the dean of journalism placed the cowl over my head.

But most of all I wanted to shake hands with the man at USC who changed my life forever—even though I never even learned his name.

This is how it happened.

11

On to Paris

I was coming to the end of my third year at USC and still having a good time. Then one morning I was drinking coffee in the Student Union when a man said something that stunned me.

He said, "Are you aware that you can go to Paris on the GI Bill of Rights?"

I told him that I didn't know it.

"Yeah, if you go to school over there, they'll pay for your tuition and give you seventy-five dollars a month."

This information was given to me at the very moment the citizens of New York State had voted to present all their sons and daughters with a war bonus. Mine came to two hundred fifty dollars, which was a vast amount of money for the time.

The check arrived in May of 1948 and I took it up to the *Daily Trojan* and showed it to everybody. Some buddies suggested I give it to the alumni fund, while others thought I might get my money's worth if I took a USC coed up to San Francisco for the weekend. There were other suggestions, such as putting it toward a down payment on a Studebaker, or buying a house in Malibu. I waited for a lull and then announced that I was going to buy a one-way ticket to Paris. I told them that my dream was to follow in the steps of Hemingway, Eliott Paul, and Gertrude Stein. I wanted to stuff myself with baguettes and snails, fill my pillow with rejection slips, and find a French girl named Mimi who believed that I was the greatest writer in the world.

I declared that Southern California was not for me. I would turn my back on Hollywood, a place that was waiting for me to write an Oscar-winning film starring Joan Crawford and Gene Kelly.

My *Daily Trojan* buddies stood around agape as I declared that I would rather live in a garret in Montparnasse than swim in a kidney-shaped pool in the Hollywood Hills.

I knew what they were thinking. How could someone as talented as I was go to Paris instead of setting up shop at MGM in Culver City? But I finally made such a good case for sin and debauchery that several of my fellow students decided to go, too.

In later years, I realized that I didn't miss much by waiving a college degree. Those friends who had majored in journalism stayed behind, and after receiving their diplomas, wound up as spokespersons for the gas company or achieved greatness by becoming troubleshooters for the post office. I have never regretted the move to France. Hollywood is a director's town—Paris was made for writers.

I said good-bye to everyone at the boarding house, including Mrs. Liebschen. There was no Flossie to bid farewell to, although I must admit I did have a fantasy of her on her knees in front of the USC library, tearfully saying, "Please don't go,

Arthur. Paris will eat you alive and spit you out. You'll never come back the innocent wonderful person you were when we bundled on the golf course at Bretton Woods."

I saw myself patting her on the head and saying, "Flossie, I'm a writer and I have to go to Paris or no one will believe it. I'll come back—even Hemingway came back."

"But what about the children we're going to have and the seven-bedroom house in Pasadena?"

I held her tightly. "All in due time, Flossie—all in due time."

I started to hitchhike from L.A. to New York. I might mention here that during my years at USC I thumbed across the country many times. But I wasn't one to stand on the highways and stick my thumb out for the better part of a day. The highways in those days had stop signs and red lights. I always stood at one, and when cars stopped I would yell, "Are you going to Tulsa?" It caught the drivers by surprise, and most of the time they would say either yes or no. If they said "yes," I would open the car door and get in, pretending that their "yes" was my ride.

It worked every time. One reason I was never turned down was because the driver had a chance to size me up when he stopped, which he didn't have when he whizzed by on the highway. On occasion, I was picked up by the police, but after they ran a check on me they let me go.

Some of my rides were not dull. I had one torrid adventure with a lady schoolteacher somewhere in Nebraska, and it lasted all the way to St. Louis. On this trip I was staying at a motel in Warren, Ohio, when a lady in the next cabin started screaming that she had been raped. The men with her insisted she was screaming because she wanted to be paid more for her services than they had given her.

Someone called the police, and the officer looked at me and said, "Did you see it?"

"No," I said, fearing I would wind up a material witness in Warren for ten years. I said, "I think a truck woke me up."

They wrapped a blanket around the woman and took her away. The men in the cabin looked at me and I immediately thought, "Time to go." I climbed out the back window with my bag and headed for the highway.

Thirty years later, I was booked to speak in Warren, Ohio, and my first thought was that the men I had seen that night would recognize me, jump on the stage, and beat me up.

When I arrived in New York, my family didn't seem particularly surprised that I was going to Paris. They had stopped being surprised at anything I did a long time ago. Besides, going to Paris seemed like a better idea than enlisting in the Marines.

My sisters and father were still living in the same apartment. Rent control was in effect, and no one could afford to move.

Edith was the first to question my intentions. "You're not going to fight in Israel, are you?" (The 1948 war had just begun.)

"No, I'm not. I'm going to Paris to become a great writer."

My father said, "Nobody makes a living as a writer."

"How do you know?"

"Shefflen's kid has been a writer for five years and he hasn't made a quarter."

"Maybe he's not a very good writer," I suggested.

"So what makes you a good writer?"

"Pop, someday you're going to refer to me as 'my son, the writer.' "

He didn't say anything but went back to reading the *New York Post.*

I believe that one of the reasons my father never engaged in any discussion with me about my profession was that in the beginning he didn't believe in anything I wanted to do. He was afraid that I would fail, and therefore he didn't want to encourage me in a career which rarely paid off for those who aspired to it.

This does not mean that when I had a syndicated column and became well known, he wasn't proud of what had been accomplished. He was simply unable to tell me. He told my sisters and he told his customers and he didn't hesitate to let on that we were related. But a wall from childhood separated us and he never could say, "Well done."

Someone once told me that it was not unusual in a father-son relationship for the father to find it impossible to praise his son. I responded angrily, "I don't care if it's usual or unusual, he could have said *something.*"

I bought a one-way ticket on a former troopship called the *Marine Jumper,* which had been turned into a student transport. In the eyes of the owners, students were in the same class as GIs, so nothing had been done to fix it up. There must have been a thousand of us on board.

When my sisters and father went down to see me off, Edith made sure the ship was not going to Israel. The crewman assured her that we were sailing to Le Havre. Ironically, there were twenty or thirty American kids on board who really were headed for Israel to fight there. They kept to themselves, and the only reason anyone suspected they were going to Haifa is they never stopped singing "Hava Nagila."

Pop had made a special trip downtown to Houston Street

and purchased corned beef, pastrami, brisket, cheeses, rye bread, cole slaw, pickles, bologna, and liverwurst—the Jewish equivalent of a light snack. I accepted it so that I wouldn't hurt his feelings. After tasting the ship's food for only one day, I blessed my father for his good thinking.

The size of his package indicated that he had not forgotten the herring they'd thrown at him on his trip to America.

I couldn't fail to make friends once we were at sea. I took up with three girls from the Parsons School of Design named Marjorie, Jean, and Maureen, and two brothers named Gelb, whose father, I later found out, owned the Clairol Company. Dick Gelb, the elder of the two, eventually became chief executive of Bristol-Myers and owned a Gulfstream airplane, which is the private plane's equivalent of the 747. I was given a ride on his plane once and I sent Dick a note saying, "I don't know what this thing costs, but I would still rather be on the *Marine Jumper.*"

There was something exhilarating about going to sea again. I could lean over the rail and not worry about being killed by a Japanese torpedo or a kamikaze pilot. All I had to worry about was a weak French franc getting strong. The weaker the franc, the longer I could stay in France.

My image of France was a country that had no toilet paper, Kleenex, or silk stockings. Ex-GIs had told me to load myself down with all the basics of life, such as soap, perfume, and canned Campbell's soups. I did as I was told. As it turned out, when I got to France no one I met was interested in the stuff. As far as I'm concerned, the day you couldn't exchange a pair of nylons for a kiss on the Place de la Concorde was the day the war was officially over.

On board ship, the major topic of conversation was careers. Whenever someone questioned me as to my plans for the future, I would say, in a voice full of mystery, "I'm writing a novel." It worked perfectly, because people assumed that good writers didn't like to talk about the books they're working on. All they would say was "Oh."

One night it was too hot to sleep in my cabin and I came out on deck at two o'clock in the morning. The moon was bright and it lit up the sea. The ship sailed smoothly through the water and I had an unbelievable surge of happiness.

I started adding up everything that had happened to me since my birth—I was not twenty-three and had lived in eight different kinds of homes with God knows how many strangers. I hadn't graduated from high school or college, but I had no fear that this would be an obstacle to a writing career.

I had survived all the pain of childhood, and after running away to join the Marines, I had made it through World War II without a bruise. Luck and chutzpah played important parts in all of it.

At this stage of my life, staring out at the peaceful water, I was as free as I would ever be.

And I was heading toward Paris—every young writer's dream. The elation was so great that I couldn't sleep, so I just looked out from the rail until dawn.

I reviewed the past with pleasure. But that morning, even in my wildest dreams, I could not foresee how wonderful the future would turn out to be.

Le Havre was my first glimpse of France. I didn't know it at that moment, but Paris would become my second home for fourteen years. It was a strange union. I spoke absolutely no French when I arrived and I didn't speak fluently when I left. Some of it was because I had no gift for learning French, or any foreign language. I managed to get along so well in Franglais, which I developed early in my stay, that I had no incentive to perfect my French. People still can't get over how badly I speak it, but there is nothing anyone can do about it.

We disembarked at Le Havre and caught the boat train for Paris. I took Marjorie, Jean, and Maureen in hand and they were very grateful for my company on the train into Paris.

The girls were apprehensive, and with good reason. In those days, Americans were told by their friends that the water in Paris was no good, the food was not clean, the milk was not pasteurized, and the French people were either hostile or drunk all the time.

The boat train arrived in Gare du St Lazare at ten o'clock at night, and the four of us marched out into the street. I found myself their leader.

"I will look after all of you," I said, very importantly, "but you must obey me."

They nodded and I went across the street from the Gare and into the first "hotel" I saw. We signed up for three rooms at a dollar a night. While we were unpacking, we saw a lot of traffic in the hall. Ladies in slips going in one direction, men in their underwear going in the other.

I tried to lighten things up by declaring, "They seem to have a very classy clientele." The girls did not laugh. I suggested we go to a French café next to the hotel. It was filled with drunken railroad workers. Finally, Jean burst into tears and said, "My first night in Paris and I'm eating in a gin mill and sleeping in a whorehouse."

I went to bed and was awakened at three o'clock in the morning by a commotion out in the hall. I opened the door and saw a naked Oriental man knocking on doors. I went back to sleep. The next morning at breakfast, I said to my three lady friends, "Did any of you see a nude Chinaman running down the hall?"

Jean burst into tears again.

My duty as their protector was to deliver all three girls to the American Express office at the Place de l'Opéra and get on with the job of becoming another Henry Miller or Gertrude Stein. I did just that, and then tanked up on water, as I was told by one of my sister's boyfriends that the only safe spots for drinking water were the American Express office and the U.S. Embassy.

Unbelievable as it may seem now, for several days every time I got thirsty I made special trips to either building. I was finally persuaded that French bottled water was okay and French tap water would not endanger my health.

Once I deposited my charges, I went to seek some temporary lodging for myself. I had the name of a tiny hotel across from the Opéra Comique and it was in walking distance of American Express. But I got slightly confused, and a French priest asked in sign language if he could help me. I showed him the slip of paper and he indicated I should follow him. Though we had no common language, I was amazed that a priest would go out of his way to help a foreigner.

When we arrived at the hotel, I stuck out my hand to thank him. But he mimed the smoking of a cigarette. I got the message and took a carton of cigarettes out of my luggage and gave him a pack. He held up two fingers to indicate he wanted two packs. The man was desperate. I gave them to him, and he went away happy that he had done the Lord's work to help a stranger find an inn for the night.

I could not afford to stay too long at the hotel because, while it was cheap for tourists, it was expensive for me. The only thing that was inexpensive was *steak au cheval.* I thought it was great until someone informed me that it was horsemeat.

I arrived at the end of June 1948, and contacted one of the

kids I had hung around with at P.S. 35. His name was Buddy Plate and he was a wild abstract artist who later became successful and had his work sold by a gallery on 57th Street. His brother had given me his address before I left the States. Buddy was a dear man (I say "was" because he passed away several years ago), and when I contacted him he offered to rent his girl's apartment to me for five dollars a month. The flat, which consisted of a dining room and a bedroom, had a toilet outside down the stairs. It was shared by other tenants on the floor. There was no bath. Buddy explained that I would be living in a working-class neighborhood above Place Clichy.

He said I could have the apartment for two months. It was a wonderful introduction to Paris. No one for miles around spoke English. When I went to the stores, I pointed to everything I wanted, and the clerks laughed as they tried to guess what I really needed.

It was summer—so all the windows were wide open and you could hear everybody in the neighborhood yelling at everybody else. The woman on the floor above woke me up every morning by screaming obscenities about her husband's mistress. In a week, I became part of the neighborhood and was accepted by everyone on the street. One reason was, since no one had a private bath in his or her apartment, we all went to a public bath around the corner. For thirty cents we were given a small cake of soap and a towel. Then we sat on wooden benches, as one would do in a doctor's office. Since I couldn't speak French, I combined sign language and my own form of Franglais, which included laughing a lot, and this seemed to please the Parisians very much. The other bathers not only put up with me, but they decided that since I was not too proud to take a bath with them I was not one of those American snobs who washed himself in a bidet at the Ritz.

Once I moved into the flat, my first step was to apply for the GI Bill at the Veterans Administration located in the U.S. Embassy. One of the most popular schools in Paris for foreigners to attend was the Alliance Française, an ancient dirty stone mansion located on the Boulevard Raspail. The school was attended by a motley gaggle of ex-GIs, many of whom made up for the lost sleep by dozing in the classrooms. Once the paperwork at the Veterans Administration was finished, I went over to the Alliance and applied for admission. It was as difficult to get into the Alliance as into the Galleries Lafayette department store.

I rode back and forth on the Metro, a miraculous form of transportation which was clean, fast, and safe. I only mention this because the French have always been ridiculed for their technology. For a while, we Americans were way ahead of them, particularly with telephones and public utilities. But they spent a lot of money on education and modernizing the country, and even with fierce ultra-left and -right political labor unions, they became the best engineers in Europe. When people scorn French architecture, I remind them that when it comes to building achievements, no one has ever duplicated the design of a French sidewalk café.

The sidewalk café is the real reason so many writers come to Paris. You can sit there for hours on end talking about good authors and bad authors, and the lovers of great women writers and writers who had no lovers and therefore wrote about the subject so much better. Anyone to your right or left at a sidewalk café was fair game for a discussion. If you were desperate, you might even start a conversation with a tableful of tourists who were looking for the "Left Bank ambiance."

A friend named Guy McLean and I made up a game when we sat at a café. We would zero in on a stranger sitting at another table and create a story about him or her. It went like this:

"You see the son of a bitch over there drinking Pernod by himself? I think he's a pimp."

"He looks rotten," I said. "I'd like to pull his chair out from under him."

"Here's what I believe. There is a poor girl screwing her brains out somewhere around here—and when she's finished she has to bring the money to him."

"Then he will make her walk home."

At that moment, an old lady might come by and take the other seat at the stranger's table.

"That's his mother. The pimp won't even go see his own mother. She has to come to see him."

"She must be so ashamed of what she raised. You would think that the least he would do is buy her a beer and a hard-boiled egg."

"Filth—that's all they have at this café—nothing but filth."

And so the game continued until we both lost interest.

The Left Bank sidewalk cafés were more interesting than the Right Bank because the people sitting at the tables had more interesting stories to tell. I was once introduced to a heavily rouged American girl who revealed that she attended Smith College. "I tried to get a job with the Marshall Plan," she told me, "but they wouldn't have me, so I am now writing porno books for Girodias. I write under the pen name Anna Klaus."

"Is it difficult?" I asked her.

"It was at first, because I made them too dirty. Girodias made me tone the stories down. I could only have a screwing scene on every third page."

She told me she got five hundred dollars a book, and no royalties.

I wish I could tell you that she turned out to be one of our greatest writers and later spent all of her royalties buying up the erotic books she'd written in her youth, but I have no idea what became of her.

There is a great deal of heartbreak at sidewalk cafés. One day at the Dome, a friend named Art Kaplan pointed out a prostitute sitting at a table. He knew her, and he thought there was a movie in her story. He told me the following tale.

A wealthy American father had come to Paris and asked Art if he could find a hooker for his nineteen-year-old son. The father said, "I've ignored him all his life, so I want to make it up to him by getting him laid." But the father wanted to make sure the son never found out that the hooker was being paid to make love.

Art called up the girl and explained the deal. She agreed. She dressed up like a college student and showed up at the Ritz for drinks. Both father and son approved of her, and the boy went out on the town with his French date.

"Now," Art said, "this is where it gets interesting. Five o'clock in the morning, the son crashes in on his father and announces that he is in love. He says that she is the most wonderful girl in the world and he's going to marry her."

"Jesus," I said.

"Eight o'clock in the morning, the father is screaming at me, 'The kid's in love with the hooker.'"

"I screamed back, 'Yeah, and she's in love with him. She doesn't want any money.'"

"It is a movie," I said, "or at least a novel. What happened then?"

"The father received a telegram that his factory burned down in Hartford, and the kid and the old man were on the next plane back to the States."

We all got mad at Kaplan. "What kind of ending is that for a story?" I yelled at him. "You're a writer. You're supposed to have figured out some way for the kid to tell his old man to bugger off and then he'd come home with the girl."

Kaplan was hurt. "What I told you was true."

"Who needs truth," said Phil George (a friend from USC), "if we're going to sell it to the movies?"

"How about the girl is at the airport crying her eyes out as the kid walks up the steps of the plane? The door closes and the engines rev up. Suddenly the door opens again and the young man rushes out and into the arms of the girl. They embrace and walk toward the Eiffel Tower."

"That's a great story," Art said. "We'll get Leslie Caron to play the girl and Mickey Rooney to play the boy."

"Humphrey Bogart would play the father."

He nodded his head in the direction of the prostitute. "Unfortunately, she hasn't spoken to me since."

Just then, the young woman stood up, and—I don't know if it was my imagination or not—but she seemed to look at us, and there was something terribly sad about her face. Suddenly, there was no Leslie Caron, and no Mickey Rooney to rush down the airplane steps into her arms. Just a girl, alone, and getting ready to go to work in a world she'd almost escaped.

The summer had drawn to a close, and it was time to leave my working-class garret and move on. Buddy was coming back with his Communist girlfriend. But my two months' stay there had changed my life. Thanks to the public baths with the

French I would never bathe the same again. So I said farewell to the Clichy neighborhood.

I found new lodging on the Boulevard Montparnasse. My friend Phil George told me about it. It was called the Hôtel des États-Unis, and had been given by the French to a group of Polish veterans who'd fought with the Allies in World War II. It was extremely cheap—seven dollars a week—with a bath, almost, on every other floor. For many people, this would have been considered roughing it, but as a veteran of Parisian public baths, I felt that I was moving up in the world. My room looked out on a brick wall of the next building. It had a sink, a bed, a desk, and a very weak light bulb. We had a Polish maid who cleaned up and supplied a weekly towel.

If I had anything to complain about, it was that the walls were very thin. I was aware of this because I lived next door to a Spanish dancer. I will never forget her screams of passion penetrating my wall. One particular morning at two, I woke up to groaning and moaning from the next room—then I heard *click, click, click,* and then more groans. Finally, a man's voice screamed, "For Christ's sake, put down those goddamn castanets."

There were about twenty rooms in the hotel, mostly filled with American ex-GIs. The focal point was a bar and sidewalk café which featured bad Polish food. The Polish owners were very sensitive about the remarks we made concerning their food, and felt it was unfair for us to compare it with all the French restaurants around us, because when it came to cooking, the Poles had gotten a late start—like a thousand years.

We were a merry bunch in the hotel. We stayed up all night drinking Pernod and beer, listening to a Polish piano player, arguing about Hemingway or Proust, or comparing Scandinavian girls to those in Kansas City. Hemingway had had a girlfriend he'd written about in the thirties named Kiki who was still alive and lived in Montparnasse. When she got drunk, she danced on the tables. She didn't look as good to us as when Hemingway had written about her, but she represented an era when the old man was king, and therefore everyone treated her with respect and kindness.

In retrospect, although my early days in Paris were crazy and insane, they did not seem as special to me then as they do now. We were as unfettered as we would ever be. We had enough money to get by, and we had no responsibilities. We fell in and out of love and we talked an awful lot with one another at the sidewalk cafés. Paris was Paris, and no one seemed to judge anybody else. People came and went; one day they would be at the Dome, and the next thing we knew they were climbing the Matterhorn.

I have always been somewhat resentful when people refer to the thirties as the golden age for Americans in Paris, as I believe that the forties, fifties, and sixties were just as golden. We had our writers, such as Richard Wright, Peter Matthiessen, George Plimpton, William Styron, Mary McCarthy, James Baldwin, and Irwin Shaw. John Steinbeck lived there for a while, as did the poet Allen Ginsberg. *The Paris Review* was a thriving outlet for unpublished Americans. Unlike the American artists of the thirties, we were not living during a Depression. We had come out of the war with great optimism. We were young and we were lucky enough to be part of a France recovering from its wounds. It was a glorious period, and I looked forward to waking up every morning, even though most of the time it was around noon.

I was getting edgy doing nothing but living it up, when I met a seventy-year-old man named Maxime de Beix. He was the stringer for *Variety,* the American show business journal, and filed stories to New York on the film and stage business in Paris.

His name had not always been de Beix. It had been Levy. But when the Germans had entered France, a family named de Beix had adopted him at the age of sixty so that he wouldn't be sent to a concentration camp. Max was the legman for New York, and I became the legman for Max. The job paid eight dollars for a column, and it took thousands of words to fill one. Working for *Variety* gave me an entry into another world. I received invitations to cocktail parties where I filled up on hors d'oeuvres so that I didn't have to buy dinner. I was welcome in French and American film offices. I even reviewed French films for *Variety.* I never gave a French film a bad review. The reason was that I lived in dread that the producer would find out how poor my French was and complain to the *Variety* editors. No one has ever questioned the credentials of a critic who writes a rave notice.

There was a lot of jealousy at the Hôtel des États-Unis when I started working. It just wasn't done, if you were on the GI Bill and lived on the Left Bank. One Saturday, I was in the bar of the Hôtel des États-Unis sitting around with some of my fellow guests when I was called to the phone. "This is Billy Rose and I'm in Paris with my wife Eleanor. Abel Green [the editor of *Variety*] said to call you when I got to town."

I immediately figured that I was being set up by my companions, so I replied, "Well, eff you, Billy Rose, and Eleanor, too." Then I hung up.

I returned to the table and said, "Nice try, guys."

They all looked innocent, with good reason. They were innocent. The person on the other end of the line was the real Billy Rose, and at the time he was one of the most important people in show business. But he was a mean person with lots of enemies, and I found out later he spent his time in Europe trying to remember what he had done to me to make me so mad at him. When he returned to New York to report his conversation, I received a tough letter from Green saying that if I ever treated one of his friends like that again, I would be out on my keester.

My *Variety* work didn't make me enough to earn a living, though, so I was always on the lookout for other jobs. That fall, I found one—but thank God I didn't get it.

Things were rolling along in Paris at that moment. The Marshall Plan had been inaugurated by Harry Truman, and its headquarters had been established in the French capital. The Marshall Plan was a way of getting Europe back on its feet. The United States financed equipment and the skills to the Western countries involved in World War II. It was an inspired program and it worked. Averell Harriman was head of it and he attracted outstanding people from all walks of life to administer the program.

What made it exciting for us was that the Plan needed Americans living in Paris for all sorts of menial positions. The positions not only paid well, but, better still, entitled you to PX privileges and housing allowances.

One day, someone came back and announced that he had landed a job in the mail room. Others acquired positions as guards and clerks. I heard that they were looking for a mimeograph operator, so I went down to apply for it. Unfortunately, a friend of mine named George Anderson had read a book about mimeograph machines, and Marion Foley, the personnel officer, gave the job to him.

I always suspected that Anderson wound up printing all the money in France. The remainder of the residents at the Hôtel des États-Unis were quickly promoted to such jobs as telling the Dutch how to make chocolate, the Danes how to make cheese, and the Benelux countries how to improve their coal and steel industry.

If there is one single person I owe for my career as a journalist, it's the blessed Marion Foley, who refused to give me a job with the Marshall Plan when I so badly needed it.

Instead, I was forced to keep looking, and my eye kept coming back to the office of the *Herald Tribune*. Every young journalist's dream was to work on the Paris *Herald Tribune*. As far as I know, it still is. At that time, the *Tribune* was located at 21 Rue de Berri, a block off the Avenue des Champs-Elysées. It had been started a hundred years ago by James Gordon Bennett, who had been banished from the United States for peeing in a piano. He wound up in France—a playboy and a great publisher.

In Europe in those days, most newspapers were either owned by, or in debt to, a political party. The *Tribune* was an American paper with no ax to grind, and people trusted it. This, by the way, has not changed. The integrity of the *Trib* is its greatest treasure. Every day, it was sent out to nineteen countries throughout the European continent, and it was the American tourists' lifeline to the motherland. (Now, through satellite, it's published all over the world.)

With the exception of the period of the German occupation, for 102 years it published stories and news features. The glamour that had sprung up around it made a job on the Paris *Trib* the most coveted of all journalism positions.

Getting a job on the Paris *Herald Trib* was hard, and required a lot more strategy than it had to acquire a job at Paramount Pictures. For one thing, no one at the paper knew Father Murphy.

I had been reading the *Tribune* every day, and it dawned on me that it was very weak in providing a valuable service for tourists. I thought that what the paper needed was a food and wine critic and someone to review films. I also planned to use my credentials as a stringer with *Variety* to get my foot in the door.

I plotted how I would approach the editors. I didn't think that three years in the Marine Corps, and three years drinking coffee at USC in the Student Union, would convince them that I should be the show business critic of the paper.

So I had to demonstrate that I had a natural palate for French food, hinting, but never saying, that I had an intimate acquaintance with the Cordon Bleu school and various Burgundy and Bordeaux wine establishments.

As a student of film, I was prepared to discuss films such as *The Birth of a Nation* and *The Blue Angel* so that they would be aware of the kind of film critic they were getting. I'd offer to start at one hundred fifty dollars a week, with the understanding that at some future date I would receive five hundred.

As I saw it, we would dicker for an office and a secretary. And, of course, I wanted an open-ended expense account.

Having worked out my strategy, I went down to the *Trib* and asked to see Eric Hawkins, a feisty little Englishman who had been a prize fighter in his youth. He had been on the newspaper for forty years and was a legend.

The editorial room where I found Hawkins was located on the first floor. The *Trib* offices could not have been better designed by a film art director. For one thing, the floors sagged, and when the presses were running, they shook. The furniture was a mixture of pre-war and neo-German occupation—mostly gray and very, very ugly.

I could tell when I walked into his office, however, that Hawkins planned to throw me out. I made my pitch to write the columns, and when I'd finished, he said, "We're not interested and, even if we were, we wouldn't hire you to write it. Now get out of here."

Some people might interpret this as a rejection. I saw it as a challenge. A few weeks later, I heard that Hawkins had gone back to England on home leave. I decided to give it another try, and went back to the *Trib* and asked to see Geoff Parsons, Jr., who was then the editor, and the man hired by the New York *Herald Tribune* in New York to run the Paris operation.

I said, "Mr. Hawkins and I have been talking about me writing a night-club column. If you let me cover entertainment and restaurants, it will encourage advertising for the paper."

Advertising. I had pushed the magic button.

Parsons said, "Could you write two columns for twenty-five dollars a week?"

"No problem," I replied. "I'm making a bundle on *Variety,* so I'll use your money for taxis."

We shook hands, and I danced like Gene Kelly out of his office, down the stairs, and along the sidewalk to the Champs-Elysées.

A few weeks later, Hawkins came back from vacation and found me sitting at my desk typing away—with a big grin on my face.

He was ticked off, but he soon got over it, and we became very close friends up until the time he passed away.

They gave me a desk as soon as Parsons hired me, which faced a blind window that opened into an airshaft covered with black soot.

My first day on the job, I looked at my typewriter, then lit a cigar, and put a clean sheet of paper into the machine.

For a while, I just sat there staring at it. I didn't want to write a column; I wanted to write a letter to all the people I had known growing up. That included my father, my sisters, my foster parents, the HOA social workers, Mrs. Egorkin, Flossie, Corporal Bonardi, and the hundreds of other people who had touched me during the early years. What I wanted to say was, "Guess who is in Paris and working on the European edition of the *Herald Tribune?*"

But instead I started to type:

PARIS AFTER DARK
BY ART BUCHWALD